T0324314

Places of Engagement

This portrait of Bert van der Zwaan was painted by Ans Markus as a present from the university on the occasion of Van der Zwaan's departure as Utrecht University vice-chancellor. The portrait will be placed in Utrecht University's ceremonial hall in the historic city of Utrecht. Photo: Lize Kraan.

Places of Engagement

Reflections on Higher Education in 2040 – A Global Approach

Edited by
Armand Heijnen and Rob van der Vaart

AUP

Cover design: Klaas Wijnberg
Lay-out: Crius Group, Hulshout

AUP is an imprint of Amsterdam University Press.

Amsterdam University Press English-language titles are distributed in the US
and Canada by the University of Chicago Press.

ISBN	978 94 6372 670 2
e-ISBN	978 90 4854 365 6 (pdf)
e-ISBN	978 90 4854 366 3 (ePub)
DOI	10.5117/9789463726702
NUR	740

Table of Contents

Part 3   Reflections on learning and teaching

Part 4   Reflections on the global and the local

Part 5   Reflections on institutional logic

Foreword

Bert van der Zwaan was Rector Magnificus (vice-chancellor) of Utrecht University from April 2011 until April 2018. He is a professor of geology who had already made major contributions to Utrecht University before he became vice-chancellor — as vice-chairman of the so-called 'Bachelor Master Committee' that created Utrecht's educational model, a model that inspired many other higher education institutions; as the initiator of impressive international research coalitions; and as the dean of the university's Faculty of Geosciences.

As vice-chancellor, he took various initiatives to further develop and bring more depth to Utrecht University's educational model. Examples of this are the complete revision of the graduate phase across the university, the initiation of a new programme of lifelong learning, a strengthened focus on evidence-based teaching and learning innovations, and new initiatives for the professional development of academic staff and for teacher careers. Bert van der Zwaan promoted the importance of excellent education not only in national networks and forums but also internationally. He believes that the League of European Research Universities (LERU), of which Utrecht University is a member, should excel not only in research but equally in the high quality of teaching and learning. In 2016, he became President of the LERU.

At a more reflective level, Bert van der Zwaan expressed his vision of the future of higher education in his book *Higher Education in 2040 — A Global Perspective* (2017). He based this book not only on the study of trends and their impact on universities worldwide but also on conversations with a large number of higher education leaders and other experts in North America, Asia, Africa, and Europe. The book has contributed in important ways to the ongoing debates about the future of higher education not only in the Netherlands but also in many other countries.

Utrecht University is very grateful for Bert van der Zwaan's leadership. He was a colleague and a leader with seemingly boundless energy, a very deep knowledge and understanding of academia from the level of local detail to the broad international picture, a vision of and an eye for institutional strategy, and excellent networks both local and global. He was always inspiring and innovative and always serving the interests of students, faculty, and staff. The initiative to publish this collection of essays is one way in which we want to express our gratitude to him. Written by colleagues and international education experts who reflect on themes that Bert touches upon in his book *Higher Education in 2040*, this volume can be considered the next step in the discussions about the future of our great institutions of higher learning.

Annetje Ottow and Anton Pijpers
Executive Board of Utrecht University

Introduction

Rob van der Vaart and Armand Heijnen

Some universities offer graduate programmes in Futures Studies: the University of Turku in Finland, the University of Stellenbosch in South Africa, or Tamkang University in Taiwan, just to mention a few. The University of Houston has an MSc course in Foresight. Aarhus University in Denmark offers Corporate Foresight at the graduate level. And there is much more. But programmes in futures studies are certainly not mainstream in the higher education landscape. Although the field has a low profile in academia, the domain of Futures Studies has many of the assets of any accepted field of knowledge: journals, conferences, professional organizations, and, more importantly, a conceptual basis and research methods (see, for example, the classical texts by Wendell Bell 1996). Futurists speak about possible, probable, and preferable futures; engage in forecasting and trend analysis as well as in scenario design and 'backcasting'; or study the worldviews and assumptions underlying people's images about futures. Maybe it is a handicap for the development of their field that there is so much 'pop futurism' around — popularized writing about the future of practically everything, from work to sex and from leisure to school — not to mention Hollywood science fiction or the gurus of utopian vistas of green, technologically advanced or otherwise healthy and happy futures.

This made it all the more courageous of Utrecht University's vice-chancellor Bert van der Zwaan to dive into the future and write his book *Higher Education in 2040 — A Global Approach* (2017). There is always the risk when making a book about the future of becoming the victim of prejudice and being accused of pop futurism, preaching, bias, utopianism, or moving beyond the requirements of academic rigour. But Van der Zwaan designed his book in such a way that all such criticism would be unjustified. He presents a thorough analysis of societal trends that have an impact on higher education: trends in the global economy and in politics, such as the global shift and a changing balance between state and market in our current neoliberal climate; technological trends, in particular the rise of information technologies and their multiple effects on education; social trends such as polarization and increased civic disengagement. He sketches the effects of such trends that are already visible in higher education and makes reasoned guesses about what will happen next when these trends continue to make an impact. He does not design scenarios of different possible futures depending on how trends will evolve in the coming decades. In our view, he remains close to the probable future and gives his vision of how to keep the probable future situation of universities as close as possible to the preferable situation of universities: as essential and preferred places of learning — in the interaction with students, in research, and in community engagement. Van der Zwaan believes that this will require drastic changes that involve radically diversifying higher education systems with flexible offerings of programmes and courses including provisions for lifelong learning, giving a central place to societal needs in research and study programmes, developing new types of coalitions with external partners, offering a campus experience that is relevant for the student's personal development, making a difference in the city or region where the institution is located, et cetera. All this is not only based on personal experience and literature but also on many interviews conducted with peers and other higher education specialists in Europe, North America, Asia, and Africa.

Van der Zwaan's contribution to our thinking about the future of higher education is inspiring and thought-provoking, but we should keep in mind that the diversity of voices and visions with regard to this topic is enormous, as is the case for any issue related to the future. Discussion requires a diversity of perspectives and visions, and therefore we will give a few recent examples of publications and events that have a different focus than the one in Van der Zwaan's book. To begin with, the New York Times sponsored a Higher Ed Leaders Forum in June 2016, which was attended by many academic leaders from the United States.[1] The topic was the future of higher education. The participants were extremely worried about the problem cluster of affordability, access, equality, and completion. This cluster of money-related issues dominated the discussion completely, followed by the issue of digitalization and how it revolutionizes thinking about the classroom experience. The views of the participants at this forum on the future of higher education were dominated, no doubt, by the desire to obtain more substantial government funding. Preferred futures reflect how one is situated geographically, politically, and culturally.

The second example is a special article in the 2015 Christmas edition of *Times Higher Education*, in which seven academics — from vice-chancellors to lecturers and researchers — gave their ideas about the university in 2030.[2] The visions presented in this article could not be more diverse. One author claims that because of computerization and rapid progress in artificial intelligence, very soon there might be few jobs left that require proof of academic ability. And with no students to teach, universities would have no future. Other contributors predict that technology will 'land' in universities in productive ways but not change anything substantial, or that lectures and seminars will again become key because they help to sharpen analytical skills — the skills needed most in the ever-changing labour market. A fourth contributor believes that devices will replace academic faculty, campuses will disappear, and year-round learning will replace the traditional academic calendar with its semesters. All seven contributors provide arguments and sources that underpin their vision. All ideas about higher education futures can be made plausible to an extent through the art of selecting relevant trends or sources. It is not important whether or not such futures are

1   https://www.nytimes.com/2016/06/23/education/educators-discuss-the-future-of-higher-education.html (consulted on 22 March 2018).
2   https://www.timeshighereducation.com/features/what-will-universities-look-like-in-2030-future-perfect (consulted on 22 March 2018).

realistic or will ever materialize. Their function is to stimulate our imagination and to make us think about our own preferences, and what we should do to realize them.

As a third example, we could look at relatively recent scenario studies about the future of higher education. Scenario studies start from the observation that societal trends may develop in different directions. The four OECD scenarios for future higher education, developed around 2010, are a good example.[3] Globalization as a trend might stabilize or intensify in a direction of even more openness, flexibility, marketization, and global orientation. But it is equally imaginable that so-called de-globalization will gain momentum in more and more sectors, resulting in an increased focus on the national or regional context and lower levels of openness.[4] A related but separate question is how nation-states relate to each other or how institutions function together: in a competitive mode or rather in a collaborative mode. If we take these two dimensions of global versus national and competition versus collaboration and plot them on two axes, we would get a matrix with four very different scenarios of the future of higher education. One of the OECD scenarios is 'Higher Education Inc.' (global outlook, competition) and another one is 'Serving Local Communities' (national, collaboration). The point here is that different assumptions lead to different conditions, opportunities, and threats for higher education institutions and systems. And this implies that we should always imagine futures in the plural and never a 'fixed' future that we are supposed to prepare for.

As a final element of the wider debate on the future of higher education, we would like to point out some of the recent books about the subject that give additional perspective and detail to some of the elements discussed by Van der Zwaan. In his book,

---

3   http://www.oecd.org/education/skills-beyond-school/42241931.pdf (consulted on 22 March 2018).
4   The term deglobalization is not only in fashion in comments about Trump's 'America First' agenda but a concept that has been in use in academic studies for almost a decade now. See, for example, the recent article by Peter van Bergeijk.

Van der Zwaan pays much attention to geographical variations in the current state of affairs and future perspectives of universities. He shows how trends and perspectives in higher education are partially different in various parts of the world, as a function of political, economic, or demographic conditions. Van der Zwaan's colleague at the University of Melbourne, Glyn Davis, focused on the specific case of Australia in his book *The Australian Idea of a University* (2017). He would agree with Van der Zwaan that radical diversification of the higher education system is urgently needed, along with experimentation and innovation, in order to survive in a context of fierce global competition from public as well as private providers of higher learning, both within and outside universities. Van der Zwaan also writes extensively about Asia. His observations about Asian universities and about how their mission and practices are embedded in the public and business interests of their respective national states are elaborated in much more detail in the 2017 book *Envisioning the Asian New Flagship University* by John Aubrey Douglass and John Hawkins.

This brief excursion has hopefully demonstrated that there is a significant amount of thinking and debate about the future of higher education and that Van der Zwaan's study is part and parcel of a much wider phenomenon of keen interest in and concern among key actors about future pathways for higher education institutions. The reason might be that there are so many discontinuities — in the sense of Peter Drucker's famous book *The Age of Discontinuity* (1969) — in today's world that business as usual is no longer an option. The debate about future directions for higher education is urgent and needs to be continued, particularly for the alignment of short-term and medium-term priorities and decision — such as in universities' strategic plans — with longer-term horizons. Here we come to the *raison d'être* for this volume of essays. At the end of March 2018, Bert van der Zwaan stepped down as Rector Magnificus (vice-chancellor) of Utrecht University. His 2017 book *Higher Education in 2040* has been received well and discussed intensely both within Utrecht University and beyond. Conversations with Bert van der Zwaan had made clear that he was not finished with the subject after the book was published but was eager to continue the debate. All this gave some key members of his staff — the university's Secretary-General Leon van de Zande and the Director of the Academic Affairs office Hans de Jonge — the idea that a book with reflections on *Higher Education in 2040* by academics at home as well as abroad might be a very welcome farewell gift for the departing vice-chancellor. The two initiators asked us, the editors of this volume, to develop the idea, and this book is the result.

We identified potential contributors to this collection of essays on the basis of the list of international experts who were interviewed by Bert van der Zwaan for his book, taking into account a fair geographical distribution and adding a focus on Dutch colleagues. Academic leaders and other key players in higher education in Asia, North America, Africa, and Europe (outside the Netherlands) wrote nine of the twenty essays in this volume. Among them are the (former) presidents or vice-chancellors of New York University, the University of Arizona, Nanyang Technological University in Singapore, the University of Strasburg, Helsinki University, plus other academic leaders from the University of Stellenbosch, National University Singapore, University College London, and the League of European Research Universities. Eleven essays were written by Dutch colleagues: three from sister institutions in the country, four from relevant Dutch institutions (the current and former presidents of the Dutch National Students Association, the Royal Netherlands Academy of Arts and Sciences, and the Association of Universities in the Netherlands), and four from within Utrecht University. We gave all contributors a very open assignment: to write a short essay focusing on any aspect — to be chosen by the author — of the future of higher education, preferably related to a section, point of view, or theme from Van der Zwaan's book. The result is a mosaic of themes and points of view, all of which represent valuable angles for thinking about higher education futures.

Van der Zwaan devoted the seven chapters of Part 3 of his book to 'Contours of the university of the future'. In this volume we have organized the twenty essays under five broad themes, which are loosely related to some of the chapters of Part 3 of Van der Zwaan's book. The first three essays offer 'Reflections on the core values of the university'. Sijbolt Noorda discusses autonomy, Alain Beretz focuses on the pursuit of excellence, and Carel Stolker writes about the freedom of speech. All three argue that these values are contested in practice. They contextualize the values by putting them in the perspective of current and future pressures that universities are facing or by confronting them with other — sometimes seemingly conflicting — values.

The next four essays are organized under the heading 'Reflections on core tasks'. James Kennedy focuses on the question of learning outcomes: what ought we to wish from university graduates? The student perspective comes next: Rhea van der Dong, president of a national Dutch student organization, presents some of her ideas about the student in 2040. Frank Miedema's essay is about research. The focus is on medical research but the issue is, of course, more general: to whom are we answering? To a closed academic community, or to societal needs? Joop Schippers writes about universities' role in lifelong learning, which he argues will become more important in the near future due to changes in the labour market.

Part 3 of this volume has four essays that focus specifically on learning and teaching and the changes that will be required in the coming decades. José van Dijck offers some thoughts about how universities should diversify the menu of what they offer to their students. Jukka Kola and Sari Lindblom remind us of the fact that teaching and learning in research-intensive universities should be based on what we know from research about effective learning and teaching practices. Dilly Fung rethinks the curriculum of university programmes in the light of rapid changes in student characteristics, knowledge development, and societal context. Anka Mulder focuses on information technology and asks how universities could and should be (or if necessary become) communities of learners in the digital age.

Part 4 of the book has four essays that together demonstrate the key importance of geography and geographical variation in higher education systems. John Sexton describes New York University's efforts to become a real global player, a global network university. Bertil Andersson, positioned in Singapore, sketches the rise of Asia in academia. Peter Vale offers his thoughts on the South African university and what he believes should be the specific characteristics of such a university given local conditions. Kurt Deketelaere takes us on a tour through the highly institutionalized European research and education landscape.

Finally, Part 5 focuses on current and future issues of higher education governance or, in Michael Crow's words, institutional logic. Michael Crow and his co-authors discuss 'academic enterprise' as a new institutional logic for public universities, particularly in the American context. Barbara Baarsma writes about the flexible labour market, the emergence of private as well as public providers of postgraduate training for lifelong learning, and how universities should relate to this context. Huang Hoon Chng, speaking from the Singapore context, believes that universities as institutions do not necessarily have to choose between being national economic assets and being independent centres of learning and discovery; in her opinion, the two can be combined. Karl Dittrich shows how good intentions turned into bad practices in his essay about quality assurance, and he indicates how the situation could be improved. Finally, Leen Dorsman highlights a typically Dutch aspect of institutional logic or rather the lack of it: the dual higher education system with research universities and universities of applied science.

One thing that shines through in all these essays is that the authors are passionate about their institutions or organizations and about the changes they believe should be made into the future. Engagement is an ingredient in all the contributions: engagement with students, with discovery, with the needs of our societies, with the future, and with the key role of higher education institutions in the future. That is why we chose the title 'Places of Engagement'. We hope that all the engagement and expertise of this collection of essays will not only please our departing vice-chancellor Bert van der Zwaan but also inspire many others who reflect on and discuss the future of higher education.

Bibliography

Wendell Bell, *Foundations of Futures Studies: Human Science for a New Era*, 2 vols. (New Brunswick, NJ: Transaction Publishers, 1996).

Peter A.G. van Bergeijk, 'On the brink of Deglobalisation... again', *Cambridge Journal of Regions, Economy, and Society*, 11 (2018): 59-72.

Glyn Davis, *The Australian Idea of a University* (Melbourne: Melbourne University Press, 2017).

John Aubrey Douglass and John N. Hawkins, *Envisioning the Asian New Flagship University: Its Past and Vital Future*, (Berkeley, CA: Berkeley Public Policy Press, 2017).

Peter F. Drucker, *The Age of Discontinuity. Guidelines to Our Changing Society* (New York: Harper and Row, 1969).

Bert van der Zwaan, *Higher Education in 2040 — A Global Approach*, (Amsterdam: Amsterdam University Press, 2017).

Part 1

Reflections on core values

Autonomy: A practice serving a purpose

Sijbolt Noorda

Among the many relevant themes that Bert van der Zwaan addresses in his book *Higher Education in 2040* are 'old and new core values' (pp. 185-194). He rightly notes that values are important for an organization's identity as well as for its inner coherence and external legitimacy. He predicts that universities will probably need them more than they used to. A return to old values and romantic pleas for restoration are no real options. Far too much has changed. A new balance must be struck between independence and interdependence of university and society. Universities ought to show more courage in making their own policy choices while at the same time taking much more seriously what they could and should contribute to society. I would put this as follows: less compliance, more service. It is this apparent paradox that I will elaborate upon in this essay: autonomous universities truly serving society.

In 1988, at the 900th anniversary of the University of Bologna, hundreds of rectors signed the *Magna Charta Universitatum*. Against the backdrop of centuries of European universities and in view of the growing cooperation between all European nations and the role of universities in an increasingly international society, they wanted to demonstrate the core principles of what a university should be. Utrecht University was among the very first to sign the document. The signature was put by Hans van Ginkel, one of Bert van der Zwaan's great predecessors as Rector Magnificus. As a matter of fact, van Ginkel had been among the eight drafters of the declaration. It may strike today's readers that the text uses pretty stately language to convey rather up-to-date ideas and convictions. Universities are portrayed as centres of culture, knowledge, and research to serve society. This is to be done by teaching younger generations, but it also requires considerable investment in continuing education. As a main feature of education and training, it is stated that universities must teach respect for 'the great harmonies of their natural environment and of life itself'.

To enable universities to play their part, the declaration proclaims four fundamental principles on which the mission of universities should be based. The first of these is about independence: 'To meet the needs of the world around [the university], its research and teaching must be morally and intellectually independent of all political authority and economic power'. Immediately preceding this statement, the university is described as an *autonomous* cultural institution at the heart of societies that for reasons of historical tradition and geography are organized in different ways. It seems to me that the very wording of this first principle ('morally and intellectually independent of all political authority and economic power') and the way it is wrapped in a statement of purpose ('to meet the needs of the world around it') as well as a description of international diversity ('societies differently organized because of geography and historical heritage') reveals the considerable wisdom on the part of the drafters. They refrained from making unilateral, complacent statements on the university but rather made it crystal clear that universities are *embedded* institutions. They are not self-serving entities but exist in a social setting, for the benefit of their particular environment. The university must be independent for a reason, in order to enable it to do what it is supposed to be doing and to best serve those whom it is supposed to be serving.

It is the aim of the present paper to explore the social quality of autonomy as well as its uses, and the challenges that come with it. Before doing so, I would like to point out that the very concept of autonomy refers to the practice of *self-rule* in lawmaking and decision-making. A country or an institution is autonomous if it sets its own rules and can determine its own future. This shows that autonomy implies a clear responsibility, namely to decide which rules and plans the institution needs and how to arrive at them. Autonomy refers to an activity, to nimble self-rule rather than to the condition of those who are being spared the demands and directives of others.

I promised to explore the social quality of autonomy. First I will discuss how autonomy is embedded in a social setting — or rather how university autonomy depends on a kind of social contract. The next question is: whose autonomy are we talking about exactly in the case of universities? This is about agency and ownership inside the institution. And finally — and most importantly — I will discuss the uses of autonomy. How can we discern that universities are practicing autonomy, and to whose benefit is it?

The great successes of universities have a downside. They are wanted. It is established opinion that higher learning and scientific research are the champions of modern civilization. They are seen as essential engines of development, fertile grounds for new generations of professionals, and indispensable providers of smart solutions to future questions. No wonder they are in high demand. No wonder universities grow in number and in size. No wonder external stakeholders hold universities in such high esteem, and no wonder they are keen to make universities yield the fruits of their preference. Governments, employers, product developers, students, and their families — they all clearly want something from the university that suits them. It is immediately clear that stakeholders' demands and preferences hold universities in check. The inevitable web of relations between a university and its stakeholders, supporters, and owners influences the university. These relations are governed by laws and contracts but are by no means confined to such formal arrangements. In many cases, the social setting as expressed by mutual expectations and commitments is much more influential than those formal frames. An institution that is granted full autonomy by law may nevertheless be bound and steered to a high degree by the dynamics of economic realities, political preferences, business priorities, or social diversity.

Autonomy is the *condition sine qua non* of the academy. How could we possibly do what we are supposed to be doing if we do not have the space or the freedom to inquire, to teach, and to criticize or to approve? Stakeholders — be they citizens; governments; political, religious or ethnic groups; businesses; or private owners — should realize that without autonomy, universities cannot properly function and deliver what they should deliver. *Autonomy must be granted.* And in reverse, universities should realize that they are partners in the social contract. But autonomy doesn't fall from heaven as a formal, legal privilege. And it is not carved in stone, once and for all. The social setting of higher education is a dynamic one, changing over time and defined by the power, interests, and trust of a good number of stakeholders. It is from these dynamics that a social contract, on which autonomy depends, emerges. So universities should fully, courageously, and continuously engage with all relevant stakeholders to update and uphold this contract.

Bert van der Zwaan's book is, among other things, an interesting reflection of his sabbatical readings. On page 102, he refers to Helga Nowotny's *The Cunning of Uncertainty* (2016). She explored the many faces of uncertainty, in particular its role in science and how to cope with it. Bert van der Zwaan refers to the book as an argument for scholarship as a pre-eminently uncertain process. He then concludes that:

> the university needs to be restructured completely: not only by providing different incentives, but by looking completely differently at what and who should steer the process of teaching and research. This unequivocally means that there should be more autonomy for individual lecturers and researchers, because it is there in particular that freedom and uncertainty play a role in achieving academic progress. (p. 102)

He goes on to cite Ronald Barnett's plea in *Being a University* (2011) for imaginative thinking about the university of the future beyond the entrepreneurial or developmental types: 'Barnett's "liquid university" could be an intermediary phase on the way to the university of the future' (p. 102). It may be that Bert van der Zwaan is more convinced by the concept of the 'liquid university' than Barnett himself, who finds this concept too risky and anarchic to really go for it. Whatever the case may be, they both make a valid point. The autonomy of individual teachers and researchers should be guaranteed if the claim for university autonomy is to have real meaning. After all, the primary processes of the academy — teaching/learning and research — are in their hands. And the responsibility that comes with it is part of their professional *habitus*. So university autonomy is about the university as an institution in all its parts. Thus autonomy always is relative autonomy. Both independence and constraint operate at a variety of levels: at the institutional leadership level as well as in the workplace, and at a good number of intermediate levels. This may seem a truism. Yet it is not rare that university leaders confidently profess their institution's autonomous position while academics in the workplace do not feel free at all to make crucial choices about programming and prioritizing. This is clearly not the way it should be. Values are crucial for an institution's identity as well as for its inner coherence. They cannot and should not reside with leadership alone. They must be discussed, defined, and lived to become truly shared values.

Universities set their own rules and enjoy a high degree of independence, but for what purpose? The *Magna Charta Universitatum* of 1988 clearly and simply states: 'to meet the needs of the world around the university'. Autonomy is a practice serving a purpose, a means to an end. But which end, or rather, ends? What are 'the needs of the world'? To what purpose do universities use their self-rule? To achieve what? Autonomy is little more than an enabler, offering freedoms and opportunities. *It is the use of autonomy that counts.* Such a use could be defining the mission and profile of your institution and identifying the community you want to serve. If done right, an appropriate use of autonomy will feed back into the social contract on which it is based. At this point, I see quite a challenge. Universities are wont to have very similar ideals about what a university is for, not just in theory but also in actual practice. The main risk is that a tendency to please, going with fashionable and powerful trends and stakeholders while siding with established interests and serving high achievers, will not be good enough for higher education. When comparing university strategies and profiles, one observes a high degree of uniformity and a low degree of differentiation, a high degree of imitation and very little difference. This is usually attributed to a couple of strong forces: the attractions of powerful examples (the so-called world-class university of international rankings), the traditional heritage of academic self-understanding, and, last but not least, the absence of direct rewards for being different. Some observers compare the university to animals or plants responding to their eco-system: it comes as no surprise that they respond in the same way if that way is successful. Yet this is not the full story. I shall try to explain why.

Universities are a worldwide success. As a general statement, this is true. It does not, however, mean that everywhere and at all times, everyone applauds them for their achievements. The opposite is true. There is substantial criticism from various sides and perspectives. Some find universities elitist and arrogant, others see them as quasi-corporations driven by money and moulded to the style and interests of the business world. Some reproach them for being inefficient, others for being self-serving. Their traditional role as guardians and promoters of the public good has lost much of its appeal. Such criticism should not be ignored. Among the many reasons for this criticism, the erosion of trust stands out. If academia can no more be trusted, the social contract breaks apart. This will first lead to pressure on funding arrangements, limitations to self-rule, and additional controls and audits, to be followed by the erosion of political support and a falling out of grace with donors. The usual answer to critical voices is a repetition *ad nauseam* of the worldwide success story, but this is not good enough. Even if that story could convince critics that the best students are receiving an excellent education, highly qualified researchers are producing ever-growing numbers of very good research results, and academic peers are quite satisfied with the quality of it all, even then this narrative would not be an answer to the criticism voiced. What about all the other students outside the statistical margins of 'excellence'? How to explain the high percentages of dropouts and unemployed graduates? Why is it that large parts of the electorate think that universities are not serving them? How is it that those infamous rankings measure international excellence but fail to gauge local or national benefits? Who can justify the spending of tax contributions by the many on benefits for the few?

If the social contract that grants self-rule to academia is to remain intact, its trust base must be considerably widened and strengthened. 'To meet the needs of the world' requires a practice of autonomy geared towards a diverse set of uses and purposes and a keen responsiveness to broader sets of stakeholders than the usual suspects. This brings us back to the apparent paradox: less compliance, more service. Or to put it another way: less obedience to fashions and funders, and more differentiation and variety, please. Which is, if I have understood it well, a very short summary of Bert's book.

Bibliography

Ronald Barnett, *Being A University* (New York: Routledge, 2011).
Magna Charta Universitatum (1988, see: http://www.magna-charta.org/resources/files/the-magna-charta/english).
Helga Nowotny, *The Cunning of Uncertainty* (Cambridge: Polity Press, 2016).
Bert van der Zwaan, *Higher Education in 2040 — A Global Approach* (Amsterdam: Amsterdam University Press, 2017).

The positive and fundamental value of excellence in universities

Alain Beretz

Bert van der Zwaan, as chair of the League of European Universities (LERU), has often been involved in promoting the excellence of European research universities. In this demanding task, Bert has demonstrated his personal qualities of leadership, determination, and diplomacy. This paper is a small tribute to his activities in that domain.

The quest for excellence is very often associated with competition. Speaking about competition in the academic sector can, according to the context or background, be considered either a basic value or a major problem. Academic competition has always been at the heart of academic life and is based on the central importance of competition in the research process. Researchers have always tried to be the first to find and the first to open new pathways of knowledge. However, I am not sure that the way the word competition is used nowadays really describes this strive for excellence or this quest (Beretz 2016). In fact, there are two types of academic competition: the first one is market-oriented, i.e. you compete for a 'market' such as student registration fees, or some sources of private or even public money. In this type of market-driven competition, higher education is treated as a commodity. The second type of competition is centrally concerned with the quest for excellence and does not involve any aggressive or predatory behaviour. In this meaning of the word, competition is more a basic value — a non-interested, unbiased quest for excellence. Two brief examples show that implementing excellence schemes is not straightforward and can lead to misunderstandings and tensions.

In France, universities are under a uniform rule regime, with only a single set of regulations serving a wide diversity of situations. For example, the budget allocated to universities is based on a single algorithm, whatever the specific profile of the university. Even the basic notion of 'research university' is seen as not acceptable by some unions or civil servants, precisely because it introduces diversity into the system. Following the model adopted earlier in Germany, France has launched a so-called 'excellence initiative' of pushing forward some ten world-level campuses. This has led to some misinterpretation and fears. If universities failed the competition, this failure was too often attributed to the supposed inequality and biased structure of the competition itself. The basic principle of such a competition is also being questioned by some unions, which believe it would open the door to a biased, unequal public academic system. In fact, the quest for excellence without underlying values is useless. When implementing excellence schemes of any kind, one too often points out the 'winners' and 'losers', and this perspective ends up yielding much frustration and opposition. To avoid this frustration, it is necessary that these schemes only come on top of a global academic system that ensures that all types of academic enterprises are funded and sustained at the level that they deserve. This way, the 'winners' do not steal anything from the 'losers'; they just receive an extra reward for their specific excellence, whatever the scale.

In the European agenda on research, one can always feel a tension between excellence and widening. The quest for excellence in research, which is a cornerstone of the European Union's Framework Programme, is sometimes seen to lead to an increase of inequalities in research and innovation, with certain countries lagging behind the rest of Europe in terms of scientific output. We need to avoid widening this gap, and those two notions should urgently be reconciled in order to avoid a loss of value and to ensure that the impact of EU investments in research and innovation is maximized. One possible solution would be to address this issue as a core dimension of the European Research Area, where the funding of excellence and the support of widening activities should be complementary and coordinated.

Opponents of the concept of excellence in universities often base their position on the assumption that excellence schemes will open or increase gaps, leading to segregated levels of research funding and biased student recruitment. They also assume that focusing on excellence will lead to supporting only large, world-class institutions and leave behind smaller ones, creating a first and second-tier system of universities based on their global research performance. Similarly, one could fear the creation of very stratified, watertight compartments of excellence within one single university. In all these aspects, excellence can unfortunately become a dividing force, which we can therefore name **exclusive** excellence. This is, of course, not my belief. But this is not only a matter of belief but of facts: excellence can be both distributive and inclusive. First, excellence can be a driving force with a strong spillover effect. When I was president of the University of Strasbourg, we were proud to succeed in the very competitive 'Excellence Initiative'. This led some teams in the university to receive significantly more support than others.

When presenting our first assessment report to the international jury, we demonstrated that we were able to avoid the 'more money, more problems' syndrome or the 'ivory tower' syndrome. We showed that the successful implementation of the initiative itself had been a major factor in increasing corporate identity and pride. This success brought all actors together, while it could have been a violently dividing agent. In fact, we had achieved *inclusive excellence*. In this state of mind, the excellent teams and structures can 'radiate excellence' towards the rest of the institution, and excellence can trickle down far beyond what is sometimes defined as an excellence perimeter. This can help to deepen a culture of excellence and spread group work across the various areas of the university (Bennetot Pruvot & Esterman 2016). Thus, inclusive excellence is not a race to the bottom; it is inclusion without dilution. It can combine the highest quality standards with a true sense of sharing and solidarity or '*esprit de corps*'.

Finally, excellence is not only the privilege of large, world-class universities. Observations of the results of excellence schemes in Germany and France, or at the European level with the European research council, demonstrate that pockets of excellence are to be found in a wide array of institutions and that excellence is not just concentrated in some champion institutions. The notion of *distributed excellence* has been used to describe this situation (KRASP and HRK 2017).

Universities would appear to have nothing to do with football. However, this metaphor may reveal a parallel between both worlds, as it has been said that the European Research Council was started as a 'Champion's League of Europe'. This prediction came true; but one should remember that those teams playing the Champion's League also have a responsibility to set an example, so that smaller clubs play the game with pleasure while respecting the rules. In his book, Bert van der Zwaan points out that 'there is an urgent need for a less corporate approach to managing universities' (Van der Zwaan 2017). Maybe negative perceptions of academic excellence are caused by such a corporate approach whereas, when considered a fundamental academic value, excellence may be a positive driving force that sets examples and provides less-biased incentives and rewards. In academia, excellence is not a nasty word, or at least it should not be. Excellent universities are not there to crush the competition. They have a strong responsibility to be flagships, to act as beacons and examples. This is 'what universities are for', as was stated in one of the founding papers issued by the League of European Research Universities, that Bert has so elegantly and efficiently chaired (Boulton & Lucas 2008). This is the legacy that Bert has transferred to us and that we can all be thankful for.

Bibliography

Enora Bennetot Pruvot and Thomas Esterman, *DEFINE Thematic Report : Funding for Excellence* (Brussels: European University Association, 2016). Available from: http://www.eua.be/Libraries/publication/DEFINE_Funding_for_Excellence.pdf?sfvrsn=4 [Accessed: 12 March 2018].

Alain Beretz, 'Competition as an engine for progress: a normal rule for universities', in *Legacy of Charles IV: Education and Academic Freedoms, Innovation and Open Society* ed. Veronika Hunt Safránková (Prague: Karolinum, 2016).

Geoffrey Boulton and Colin Lucas, *What are universities for?*, LERU position paper (Brussels: League of European Research Universities, 2008). Available from: https://www.leru.org/files/What-are-Universities-for-Full-paper.pdf [Accessed: 12 March 2018].

KRASP and HRK, *Distributed Excellence. A discussion paper by the German and Polish Rectors´ Conferences on elements of the future research, education and innovation funding of the EU after 2020* (2017). Available from: https://www.hrk.de/fileadmin/redaktion/hrk/02-Dokumente/Distributed_Excellence_HRK-CRASP_11_2017.pdf [Accessed: 12 March 2018].

Bert van der Zwaan, *Higher Education in 2040 — A Global Approach* (Amsterdam: Amsterdam University Press, 2017).

'Let the lightning strike!' — Free speech and the university

Carel Stolker

As Rector of Leiden University, I am often asked about non-mainstream contributions made by Leiden scholars to public and political debates.[1] On Twitter, at alumni events, or at the local market in my hometown of Leiden, concerned individuals are keen to have a quiet word with me about whichever of our professors has most recently made some controversial statement in the media. Such individuals are almost always embarrassed about the university — the very university you hope they would be proud of. But asking someone whose job it is to run a university to silence his or her professors strikes me as somewhat alien. My own university has for centuries had as its motto *Praesidium Libertatis* (Bastion of Freedom), symbolising the courage to speak truth to power. In Leiden, we put it as follows:

> Our University stands for freedom of spirit, thought and speech, and for the independent development of research and teaching. It is a safe haven where all questions can be asked and answered freely. [...] The University is committed to developing, disseminating and applying academic knowledge, and is a reliable beacon in national and international societal and political debates.

1   This is an extended version of an address by Carel Stolker, Rector Magnificus (vice-chancellor) of Leiden University, on the occasion of the 443rd Dies Natalis of Leiden University on 8 February 2018. The author wishes to thank his colleagues who provided very useful comments on earlier versions of this paper.

The paragraph about Utrecht University's core values is somewhat different. It reads:

> The university is a place where employees and students receive enough space to develop their talents. Thinking independently is a distinguishing feature of our academic community. The freedom of employees and students sets high standards for acting responsibly and with integrity: our attitude towards work is motivated, meticulous, reliable and morally justifiable. Integrity also requires an open and respectful interaction between employees and students.

Freedom of *speech* is not mentioned here as such. And it is noticeable that the acclaimed book by my good friend, outgoing vice-chancellor Bert van der Zwaan, *Higher Education in 2040 — A Global Approach*, does not mention the issue of free speech in academia either. Even so, I am sure he will have had similar experiences to my own, perhaps not at the market in Leiden but almost certainly at a similar market in Utrecht. So, this seems a good time for me to try to sketch out the bones of a new chapter for the second edition of his book. As we are all aware, in a politically divided and globalising world, free speech is a subject that will become increasingly important for Dutch universities, too. The heated debates about free speech on university campuses that are currently being conducted in the United Kingdom, and even more so in the United States, demonstrate this all too clearly. I recently read an interesting interview with British scholar Joanna Williams on this topic. I know almost nothing about her political views except that she supported Brexit. What was especially noteworthy in the interview was her comments about higher education. Particularly in the academic world, she says, controversial ideas are absolutely essential: 'They challenge you. If you disagree, you can use them to refine your own opinion. In the past, new knowledge has often been seen as offensive. Plenty of efforts were made to get rid of the theory of evolution. If the university's goal is only to give space to insights that won't offend anybody, you won't get anywhere.'[2] And American Professor Keith E. Whittington, author of a book on free speech, wrote in the Princeton Alumni Weekly: 'Embracing free speech is easy if the speech never seems very challenging. [...] It is much more difficult to learn to tolerate those with whom we disagree and who espouse ideas we find preposterous, repugnant or even dangerous.'[3] In this essay for Bert van der Zwaan, my proposition is that universities, more than any other institutions, must defend the freedom of the spoken and written word, but that we can only do this if we are prepared to enter into serious debate with all comers.

Open debate by its very nature includes people who hold different views from our own. A truly open debate not only requires the courage to conduct it but also calls for university presidents and deans to let such debates take place. Indeed, they should encourage and, if necessary, defend such debates. In addition, it calls for proper codes of behaviour and an atmosphere of safety in which views can be exchanged. After all, a university is much more a community of people than simply an organisation. As a community, it can only flourish on the basis of good mutual relations: think of our scholarly associations, our societies and academies, our institutes and faculties, all of which focus on discussion and debate. Within these communities, we strive for the utmost freedom and safety to conduct that debate. It is just such an open discussion with colleagues, students and society that makes the university more than a mere speakers' corner. For those who want to participate in the debate, this means, for example, going beyond just blogging on a site where you know in advance that everyone will agree with you, or tweeting within your own safe bubble. It also means resisting the temptation

2   In Vincent Bongers, 'My opinion is too dangerous', *Mare*, 15 February 2018.
3   Keith Whittington, *Speak Freely: Why Universities Must Defend Free Speech* (Princeton: Princeton University Press, forthcoming). This is an adapted excerpt from his forthcoming book. See also Sigal R. Ben-Porath's *Free Speech on Campus* (Philadelphia: University of Pennsylvania Press, 2017), which gives a good illustration of the many struggles that free speech produces on university campuses.

to place like-minded people on a PhD examination committee or boycotting annual meetings of your academic colleagues because they are all very much against your position. Open debate demands an open attitude. Open debate is so important because a community always runs the risk of descending into groupthink while purging out competing views. For example, there can be a tendency to mainly appoint people who are like ourselves and who think as we think. This is one reason why the increasing focus on diversity is so important, not only in terms of gender or cultural or social background, but also, and maybe above all, in terms of opinions and views.

So how can we avoid such mainstream thinking in our universities? If you are looking for the right direction to take, it is always wise to know where you are coming from. Then you discover that 'diversity of views' goes back a long time. For my own university, the concept of diversity of views has very old roots. Since its foundation, shortly before Utrecht University was established, diversity of views has always been the mainstay of Leiden's appointment policy. Even as early as the sixteenth and seventeenth centuries, the university was scrupulous in ensuring that different schools of thought were expressed in the curriculum. If an Aristotelian was appointed, for instance, this was balanced by the appointment of a Cartesian. There were at least two important reasons for the university's policy, university historian Willem Otterspeer (2008) writes. First, the clashes fuelled the debate on fundamental scientific principles, something that is crucial for a university. And second, they served as a 'lightning conductor', not preventing the lightning of debate from striking but bringing it constructively under control. This is a tradition that universities should continue to cherish today. It explains why I am so happy with my Leiden colleagues who throw themselves not only into scholarly discourse but also into public and political debates, and with the freedom that we as a university are able to afford them. For any academic institution, there is nothing so satisfying as to witness two opponents battling it out with each other in an environment that invites debate.

Many countries such as Turkey or Hungary (with regard to the Central European University in Budapest) do not have — or no longer have — this freedom for their academics.

So, let the lightning strike, I say.[4] Rectors or presidents of universities should as a matter of principle *not* interfere in the subject matter of the debate. Yet they *do* bear responsibility for shaping and facilitating that debate, and thus for keeping internal disputes under control. Without this, a true debate would be impossible, and the so highly vaunted academic community could easily fall apart. Having said this, does it mean there are no limits to what is acceptable? No, it does not. We are all bound by the limits of the law, such as not inciting hatred. Equally, we are bound by the rigours of academic integrity, which prohibits, for example, fabricating research results. And ensuring the physical safety of students and staff is a key obligation for every university. Here, yet another core value comes into play: the *quality* of our work as academics. We may quite rightly have particular expectations of those who invoke the freedom of free speech, namely that they will at all times be guided by the importance of the quality of their contributions. Whether it is a matter of a tweet, a blog, or a column, questionable conduct by academics strikes at the heart of one of academia's main tasks: to be a reliable beacon for the world. My predecessor, Paul van der Heijden, commented at length when he was still vice-chancellor at the University of Amsterdam, on the role and position of so-called 'public intellectuals' (2003a, 2003b). In his discourse, he quite rightly acknowledged his own responsibility. His issue was that columnists, for example, are in an attractive, and perhaps convenient twilight zone. Whereas scholars within academia are required to be accountable for the quality of their work, the situation is quite different outside

---

4   See also Martijn van Calmthout, 'Academics should engage more explicitly in public debate. Right now the debate needs academics, including those from the right' (in Dutch), *De Volkskrant*, 9 December 2017; as well as 'Universities Should Encourage Scientists to Speak Out about Public Issues', editorial in *Scientific American*, February 2018.

the academic arena. As Van der Heijden pointed out, there it is a free-for-all: the newspaper that publishes an article does not employ the columnists or the company that broadcasts their work; the university employs them. However, in these media appearances, members of university staff are not acting in the context of their academic position. I agree with him. There must be no question of their abusing this position.

Let the lightning strike, and control its effects. This applies not just to our own academic staff; rather, diversity of views also encompasses all those that we, including our students, want to invite to speak or write at our university. In many universities, the question today is: who do you invite and who do you ban from speaking? The University of California, Berkeley, made world headlines when it was accused of attempting to distinguish politically correct from not politically correct speakers. But the new Dean of Law there, Erwin Chemerinsky, argues in his book *Free Speech on Campus* (2017, co-authored with Howard Gillman, Chancellor at UC Irvine) that the university really has to be the forum for the new, the provocative, the disturbing, and the unorthodox.[5] Chemerinsky and Gillman quote a committee report from 1974 (a very different time!) about free speech at Yale University — the so-called Woodward Report — which concluded: 'We value freedom of expression precisely because it provides a forum for the new, the provocative, the disturbing, and the unorthodox. Free speech is a barrier to the tyranny of authoritarian or even majority opinion as to the rightness or wrongness of particular doctrines or thoughts.' There was one dissenter on the committee: Kenneth J. Barnes, a Harvard law student and graduate student in economics.[6] Barnes agreed that

5   The words 'the new, the provocative, the disturbing, and the unorthodox' are from a report of the Committee on Freedom of Expression at Yale, 23 December 1974.
6   Apparently, the debate within the committee was not always easy, as one can expect with such a challenging topic. In his accompanying letter, Chairman Woodward mentioned that Barnes' dissent was only received after the committee had finished its deliberations, completed the writing of its report, and disbanded for

free expression is an important value, which we must cherish and protect. But, he argued, whereas the majority of the committee were willing to accept the 'short-run' costs by insisting that free expression be the 'paramount' priority in a university,

> ...I would try to balance the conflicting interests in each case, and weigh the values which would be sacrificed in the 'short run' against the potential 'long-run' knowledge which might be gained by allowing the free expression. If, for example, Hitler was invited to Yale to discuss his research into the area of Aryan racial superiority, and his policy prescription of extermination of all non-Aryans, I would have a hard time justifying allowing him to speak. Even if I were confident that his theories would, if wrong, eventually be disproved in the 'long run', I have learned from history that the 'short run' costs would be overwhelming.

But Chemerinsky and Gillman do not agree. They go even further in their reasoning. They believe we should not let solidarity, community feeling, politeness, or mutual respect — important as these are— take precedence over freedom of expression. Quoting the Yale Report again:

> Without sacrificing its central purpose, it cannot make its primary or dominant value the fostering of friendship, solidarity, harmony, civility, or mutual respect. To be sure, these are important values ... but ... never let these values, important as they are, override the central purpose.

In the spirit of the rigorous content of the US First Amendment, which is much more protective of free speech (and many non-Americans would probably say this protection goes decidedly

the holidays. The committee was therefore unable to comment on the faithfulness with which its views are represented, the scrupulousness with which its words are quoted, or the accuracy of the factual allegations.

too far), this quote conveys a difficult message: never allow friendship, solidarity, community feeling, mutual courtesy, reciprocal respect, or the desire to give our students an inclusive learning environment — and the importance of all of these is undisputed — to weigh more heavily than freedom of expression.

Both the Yale Report and Chemerinsky and Gillman's book show that the issue of diversity of views at the academy, both on campus and in the relative privacy of the classroom, is not always simple. Because, similar to the risk that university communities run of appointing mainly clones of themselves, there is the danger that we are so nice and accommodating towards one another that true debate is no longer possible. Diversity and inclusiveness — two words that we so often utter in a single breath — can unfortunately at times also lead to friction. But here, too, it is right to mention the young dissenter Barnes in the Yale Report:

> [Free speech] is not the only value which we uphold, either in our society or in our universities. Under certain circumstances, free expression is outweighed by more pressing issues, including liberation of all oppressed people and equal opportunities for minority groups.

Two weeks after my own speech at Leiden University's Dies Natalis, I had an in-depth conversation with some young Leiden University scholars of colonial history; they stressed the overriding importance of inclusiveness at the university. And although I fully agree with the importance of inclusiveness (and the importance of equality), I differ from them because as a vice-chancellor I really fear the slippery slope where, indeed, the new, the provocative, the disturbing, and the unorthodox would become the victim.

This dilemma — how to underline the importance of an environment that combines both diversity and inclusiveness — may well be felt even more strongly at the campus-style universities that are more prevalent in the United States, for example. On these campuses, students — and in some cases university staff — occupy a distinct communal space. This may have the effect of making them rather more vulnerable as a community, including in terms of their social safety. Yet for every university, campus-style or not, diversity of views applies to students and their teachers, particularly in the more protected environment of the classroom. Sigal R. Ben-Porath, in her wonderful book on free speech on campus, quotes University of Chicago Chancellor Robert Maynard, who wrote in 1936 that a liberal education frees a person 'from the prison-house of his class, race, time, place, background, family, and even his nation'. To this she adds:

> Students should be encouraged to not rely solely or mainly on identity groups for political expression; rather, they should be invited to learn to extend their sense of themselves as political actors beyond their identity groups. Colleges [and universities — CS] should fulfil their civic and educational missions by protecting and encouraging political and other forms of speech by individual students and student groups. Students should not be perceived or encouraged to act in ways that insulate them from conflicting views; exposure to opposition and disagreement should not be included in the notion of harm from which students must be protected.[7]

But Ben-Porath, as a teacher and researcher at the University of Pennsylvania Graduate school of Education, also pays much attention to the importance of inclusiveness within the four walls of the classroom. Because here — in that relative intimacy — an open, wide-ranging, and inclusive atmosphere is a crucial condition for teaching and learning. In her book, she offers teachers some practical ways to plan and organise an inclusive classroom environment that is committed to the protection of

7   Ben-Porath, *Free Speech on Campus* (Philadelphia: University of Pennsylvania Press, 2017), pp. 48-49.

free speech.[8] Academic teaching, she argues, is more demanding and more limiting than the rules of pure free speech: 'Students on more liberal campuses who feel marginalized because of their conservative or other right-leaning political ideologies should sense that their views are respected and valued whether or not they are reflected in a particular syllabus. Minority students on mostly white campuses should feel the same'.[9] Yet, she continues, for the teacher it is best not to avoid controversy, neither when the professors bring it up nor when students raise controversial issues. And here, too, the lightning metaphor is a valid one: 'It is likewise important not to let the controversy get out of control, taking over the lesson plan or damaging the relationships among students or between students and their instructor'.[10] Campuses, Ben-Porath rightly says, can hardly be expected to reflect democratic practices and ideals without adapting them to their institutional context and goals.[11]

Free speech at the university, be it in class or on the wider campus, is not a given; it is something we have to work for every single day. Personally, I will try to be guided by the lessons that our university history teaches us: let the lightning strike, but control its effects and nurture good and open relations within the academic community of teachers and students. And yes, I'm sure that every vice-chancellor or university president will have difficult cases to deal with. But we have to guard against fearing 'the provocative, the disturbing, and the unorthodox' the contrary, we should welcome them. The academic world is the very place where we do not necessarily have to agree with one another, as Tilburg University Professor of Law Herman Schoordijk once said. And let us do this in an environment and in a form that make genuine debate possible — to avoid the university becoming that speakers' corner.

8   *Idem*, p. 94 ff.
9   *Idem*, p. 90.
10 *Idem*, p. 94.
11 *Idem*, p. 115.

Finally, to illustrate the point, I would like to share with you a telling experience from my university. Two years ago, American Attorney General Loretta E. Lynch, a highly respected American Minister of Justice serving under a highly respected American President, came to speak at Leiden University. As usual, our students were to ask questions following the Attorney General's speech, and one question they wanted to raise concerned the sensitive issue of the death penalty in the United States. Without the Attorney General being aware of it, just a few hours before her speech to remove this particular question. Our response was that the Attorney General would in that case not be welcome. Attorney General Lynch came, she gave her speech and she discussed the issue of the death penalty at length and in some detail. In my opinion, this is precisely how things should be at an academic institution. I have little doubt that Bert van der Zwaan will agree!

Bibliography

Sigal R. Ben-Porath, *Free Speech on Campus* (Philadelphia: University of Pennsylvania Press, 2017).

Vincent Bongers, 'My opinion is too dangerous', *Mare*, 15 February 2018.

Martijn van Calmthout, 'Academics should engage more explicitly in public debate. Right now the debate needs academics, including those from the right' (in Dutch), *De Volkskrant*, 9 December 2017.

Erwin Chemerinsky and Howard Gillman, *Free Speech on Campus* (New Haven and London: Yale University Press, 2017).

Paul F. van der Heijden, *Public intellectuals* (in Dutch). Address on the occasion of the 371st Dies Natalis of the University of Amsterdam, 8 January 2002 (Amsterdam: Vossiuspers, 2003).

Paul F. van der Heijden, *Public trust* (in Dutch). Address on the occasion of the 372nd Dies Natalis of the University of Amsterdam, 8 January 2003 (Amsterdam: Vossiuspers, 2003).

Willem Otterspeer, *The Bastion of Liberty. Leiden University Today and Yesterday* (Leiden: Leiden University Press, 2008).

'Universities Should Encourage Scientists to Speak Out about Public Issues', Editorial in *Scientific American*, February 2018.

Keith Whittington, 'Why Universities Must Defend Free Speech', *Princeton Alumni Weekly*, 7 March 2018 (2018a).

Keith Whittington, *Speak Freely: Why Universities Must Defend Free Speech* (Princeton: Princeton University Press, forthcoming, 2018b).

Bert van der Zwaan, *Higher Education in 2040 — A Global Approach* (Amsterdam: Amsterdam University Press, 2017).

Part 2

Reflections on core tasks

What ought we to wish from university graduates?

James Kennedy

Bert van der Zwaan is no defender of the ivory tower. In his recent book, *Higher Education in 2040 — A Global Approach* (2017), he has shown that the university must convincingly demonstrate its value to society, should it wish to survive into the future. His book entails a rich range of observations and prescriptions but seems to centre around two sets of ideas. One is that the university abandon its isolation by developing partnerships outside of the university as well as innovative forms that transcend classic university models, whether in the realm of IT or interdisciplinarity. In so doing, new knowledge is created in the process. And the other is that the university must focus much of its efforts on solving the rising number of problems facing society. Citizens and politicians will have increasing impatience with — and a declining willingness to pay for — a university that continues to stand at some remove from life as they live it and from their real world problems.

Some of his vision can be found, naturally enough, in Utrecht University's Strategic Plan of 2016-2020. It commits the university to educating students (and academicians) to take the lead in addressing current challenges and problems. Educationally, the university must equip students to become research-seasoned professionals. At the same time, they must be sufficiently broadly educated to comprehend the complexities of the challenges that society faces. The ability of university graduates to think out of disciplinary boxes, in this vision, not only strongly enhances their place on the job market but also enables them to serve society as innovative problem-solvers. In sum, Bert sympathetically champions the university as 'the discoverer of the sorely needed knowledge that will play an essential role in keeping the society of the future running effectively.'[1] His commitment to breaking down the divide between university and society and having the former better serve the latter is a laudable and, I hope, lasting achievement. The continuing social and political legitimacy of the university will depend on it.

One recurring question important to me — and of importance to the future of the university — is what kind of graduates we should wish to cultivate at the university. Is the innovative professional the best expression of a university education? Bert himself is certainly not at all unmindful of the need for the university to be mindful of a wider mission than the T-shaped professional. He speaks in his book of cultivating responsible citizenship through education and of stimulating ethical reflection. Indeed, as university campuses become the multifunctional social hubs of learning that he expects them to become, then they will — more than they do now — promote 'more interaction, more culture and more conviviality'. In doing so, universities 'will return to the formational task that used to characterize the university years back'.

But these wider themes remain relatively undeveloped in the book — how exactly can and should we find ways to reinvent its 'formational task'? The question is critical. Daniel Coit Gilman, in founding Johns Hopkins University, the first American research-oriented university, articulated that the establishment of such an institution 'means a wish for less misery among the poor, less ignorance in schools, less bigotry in the temple, less suffering in the hospital, less fraud in business, less folly in politics'.[2] We could add, nearly a century and a half later, any number of new topics. The point is that identifying — let alone achieving — such aims clearly requires from graduates more than knowledge and know-how but a set of dispositions that make them heedful of such issues in the first place. As the educationalist Cynthia Wells has argued: 'Without specialized knowledge, higher education

---

1   Van der Zwaan, p. 172.
2   Cited in Nelson, p. 75.

would not be able to fulfil its call to address the very pressing challenges facing our world today. Nevertheless, specialization without attentiveness to integrative questions of ethics and meaning would fail to faithfully address the technically complex but also fundamentally human dimensions of the world's deepest needs.'[3]

The topic of the 'intent' and 'purpose' (*'de bedoeling'* in Dutch) of our education now and into the future is something that a small, informal group of the community of Utrecht University has begun to explore since its first meeting in September of 2017. Calling itself the 'Acoesticum Society' after the site of its first meeting, this group, which includes not only the vice-deans of education but also graduate students and educational leaders, have met to encourage an extended conversation in the university community about the purposes of university education. No one in 'society' is of exactly the same mind about which policy prescriptions should be pursued at the university, and that is not the purpose. But there is a shared concern about several recurring themes that, with an eye toward the future, will be important for our institutions. The first theme focuses on the importance of embedding the role of the university graduates as 'problem-solvers' into a wider context of committed citizenship. It roughly parallels the sentiments of (the now retired) Harvard president Drew Gilpin Faust, who sees (in Bert's words) 'the role of the university...as an educator of responsible citizens who will make great contributions to the sustainable society of the future'. A university graduate's responsibility toward society does not end when she goes home from work but expresses itself in a continued engagement with society. This can be reflected in a strong sense of commitment to the common good. Under Bert's leadership, the 'civic university' and 'civic engagement' have received more traction, but this remains an underdeveloped theme. Yet it is important that responsible citizenship be cultivated to correct

---

3   Wells, p. 61.

not only solipsism (about which Faust is concerned) but also a narrowly technocratic approach to 'fixing' problems.[4]

The second theme is that the science of the university should be committed to cultivating a broader set of academic dispositions than can be defined by disciplinary study alone. In some ways this fits into a new emphasis, promoted by Bert, on interdisciplinarity, with its promise of putting science together in new and surprising ways. It also goes further: it means developing an academic habitus among all students that, while committed to advancing the newest insights of science and scholarship, is interested in more than its practical effects alone. An alacrity of mind, an ability to discern the wheat from the chaff in public or academic debates, a patience for struggling through complex material, and a thoughtfulness about difficult challenges are all examples of the kind of academic and moral virtues to which the university must attend and which its teachers should attempt to model. No society will give science or the university a proper place if that society has become devoid of citizens who are committed, in the widest sense, to the life of the mind. Universities undermine their own future existence if they understand their educational vocation only in terms of the products produced and not in terms of the qualities of their graduates.

Last but not least, there is sensitivity to older educational visions that call for the university to be alert to the flourishing of their students as human beings. Here, too, Utrecht University has made significant strides in recent years in a landscape in which Dutch institutions are not doing poorly from an international perspective: more attention is being given to customized education, the importance of mentors and tutors is being recognized, and a supportive learning community is being developed further. And yet considerable problems remain in a bureaucratized educational system that has very little time, inclination, and capacity for bigger questions and wonderment, for encouraging risks and their accompanying failures, or for discerning the unique talents

4   Van der Zwaan, pp. 170-173.

of our students. Inattention to the lives of our students thus undermines the whole educational enterprise. These concerns, again, are not a departure from the core emphases that Bert van der Zwaan has admirably pushed in his tenure as rector. Rather, they are supporting elements for any university that seeks to root itself more deeply in, and to interact with, society and its needs. For precisely that reason, they demand more prominence in the coming years.

Bibliography

Stephen J. Nelson, *The Shape and Shaping of the College and University in America: A Lively Experiment* (London: Lexington, 2016).

Cynthia A. Wells, 'Finding the Center as Things Fly Apart. Vocation and the Common Good', in *At This Time and In This Place. Vocation and Higher Education* ed. David S. Cunningham (Oxford: Oxford University Press, 2016).

Bert van der Zwaan, *Higher Education in 2040 — A Global Approach* (Amsterdam: Amsterdam University Press, 2017).

The student in 2040

Rhea van der Dong

Looking into the future is something scientists have yet to figure out how to do. What we can do is make educated guesses about what the future will look like. This is what Bert van der Zwaan did in his book *Higher Education in 2040*. He put a lot of research and knowledge in a crystal ball and asked himself: what would higher education look like in 2040? Considering all the changes that universities have gone through in the past centuries and the speed at which things are changing in our century, this is an intriguing question. What does the future have in store for us? In his book, Van der Zwaan tries to give some answers to this question. He mentions important challenges that universities are facing, the most important one being the decline in government funding. He also suggests some solutions to these challenges — solutions that can have a big impact on higher education, our society, and students. This last group is the one that intrigues me. When I fill my crystal ball with what I know about students and investigate 2040, what do I see? What will the future of students look like? Just like everybody else, I am not able to predict the future. But like Van der Zwaan, I can make some educated guesses. Looking into my crystal ball, I see that students face at least two threats, which I would like to call meteorites. I call them this because these threats are serious and near but not yet definite. Parts of it might have already reached us, but they could also burn up completely on their way towards us. If our atmosphere is thick enough, these meteorites will not reach us. But if we don't build an atmosphere thick enough, I am afraid that by 2040 we will be hit. And then our universities could be populated by at least the following two types of students: the privileged student and the burned-out student.

The privileged student. In my opinion, one of the main threats to higher education is its lack of accessibility. Some people might feel that this is an outdated threat. They will point to all the efforts of recent decades to make our system of higher education accessible to not just the children of doctors and dentists but also those of bakers and builders. I certainly realize that our (Dutch) system is significantly more accessible than it was fifty years ago, and I am proud of that. And that is exactly why I regard what is happening in our decade with fear. My national student organization observes many developments that can have a negative impact on the accessibility of higher education in the Netherlands. What are these developments that threaten accessibility? Looking at individual policy measures, these may not seem to be extremely alarming or problematic. From the perspective of a civil servant at the ministry of education, or in a university board meeting, the negative effect of individual new measures might seem minor and surmountable. But for the people who are facing the full package of recent policy changes, the effects are substantial. Students do not face just one hurdle but many different ones.

Let us take a closer look at these hurdles. The biggest one is a financial one. A few years ago, the Dutch government dramatically cut back its financial support for students. Instead of receiving a monthly scholarship payment from the government, students must now take out a big loan to be able to study. For most of the students, this does not have to be a problem, but for some students it is.[1] Another issue is the growing tendency to make higher education selectively accessible, something that has also been advocated by Van der Zwaan. Again, this may not pose problems for many students, but it does for those same students for whom the financial hurdle is an issue.[2] The last challenge I will mention here has to do with the growing internationalization of higher education. I am a proponent of sensible internationalization, but I find it painful to see that study abroad is often out of reach for

1   See Anja van den Broek et al. (2017) p. 170.
2   See Ministry of Education (2017) pp. 3 and 7.

those same students who slip through the cracks when it comes to the financial and selection hurdles.[3]

Our system of higher education is accessible to most students but contains hurdles for different potential student groups: students with parents who did not study themselves, students with an immigrant background, students with disabilities, and students with limited financial means. From a distance, the system might look accessible and the hurdles might seem to be solvable, but when we look at it through the eyes of these student groups, it can be a hell of a job to get in and complete a study successfully. The result of this — the erosion of equal opportunity and the squandering of talent — should be unacceptable to all of us. I am afraid that these hurdles will only grow bigger in the years ahead. Unfortunately, most of the solutions suggested for the decline in government funding affect the accessibility of our education in a negative way. This is a threat we must take seriously, because otherwise in 2040 we will have gone back in time and our universities will be populated once again by a very select group of privileged students.

The burned-out student. The second threat is one that is already approaching and is nearly upon us. For years, politicians and higher education leaders have been complaining about the lack of ambition and the lax attitude of Dutch students.[4] If we were to translate some of the policy texts into common language, it would boil down to this: students were lazy. What I see around me right now is something completely different. I see students who are experiencing an enormous amount of pressure: pressure to perform at their best, to make good and sensible choices, to not make errors, to have a perfect life to show their peers, and to live up to the expectations that society has of them. Students are also being pulled in two different directions: they must finish their studies as quickly as possible because it is prohibitively expensive to study for a longer period of time, but at the same

3   See Royal Netherlands Academy (2017) p. 76.
4   See Ministry of Education (2011) p. 21.

time they are expected to do as many extracurricular activities as possible to enhance their career opportunities. Students are often told that the labour market expects a curriculum vitae with at least one internship, a study abroad, leadership experience, extra courses, honours, a job, and a lot more. Just studying is not an option any more. Of course, some degree of pressure is not bad and is sometimes necessary, but the pressure I am talking about is too much and unhealthy. For many students, it results in mental and psychological problems. The number of burnouts has increased dramatically in recent years. This problem is well documented in research.[5]

What frightens me is that the number of students who are experiencing enormous pressure is growing rapidly. Within just a few years, this has become the number one problem for young people. That is why we need to act on it now. Looking at the speed at which burnouts and psychological problems among students have been emerging and growing, the situation might deteriorate further if no action is taken. One of the main reasons this problem is not getting the attention it needs is, I believe, the gap between generations. When I speak about this subject as a representative of Dutch students with policymakers, university leaders, or politicians, they don't really seem to understand the seriousness of this issue. Most of them — there are exceptions to this rule, of course — draw parallels with their own studies and conclude that contemporary students should not complain and just take it easy. Or they kindly bestow their insight that life is hard and that they should just get used to it. They don't seem to realize that the times and the situation for students have changed considerably. This lack of empathy and awareness is problematic: if the generation that has the power and means to come up with solutions does not see that this is a real problem, the issue will only become more and more urgent.

5   Jolien Dopmeijer 2017; Maartje Conijn et al. 2015; Wilmar Schaufeli et al. 2002; Nikki Gubbels & Rutger Kappe 2017.

With the rapid pace at which things are changing nowadays, it can feel as if we students don't have a say in it. One of the great things that Van der Zwaan shows us in his book is that this is not true and that we can influence what the future will look like. The things we do today will shape 2040. We are the ones who decide what we see in the crystal ball and how we act upon that. In the end, it is all about choices: what do we want 2040 to look like? I hope that in our journey towards 2040, in our battle with decreasing government funding, and in our efforts to improve the situation, we will not throw away what is already good. To all those people who shape the future, I would like to say: please be careful and proud of what we have, especially the accessibility of our education. Because what Van der Zwaan also shows us is that the way back from elite education is extremely difficult, if not impossible. And I hope that in 2040 students also just get to be students and enjoy that, instead of working themselves into a burnout in their effort to be perfect. I hope that in the coming years we will build an atmosphere thick enough, and that these meteorites that threaten our accessibility and mental wellbeing will burn up completely.

Bibliography

Anja van den Broek et al., *Monitor Policy Measures 2016-2017. Study choice, study behaviour, and loan behaviour in relation to policy measures in higher education, 2006-2016* (in Dutch) (Nijmegen: ResearchNed, 2017).

Maartje Conijn, Henri Boefsma, and Willem van Rhenen, 'Burnout among Dutch students in medicine: Prevalence and causes' (in Dutch), *Nederlands Tijdschrift voor Geneeskunde* 159 (2015).

Jolien Dopmeijer, *Study Climate, Health, and Study Success. Monitor FIVE Programme* (in Dutch) (Zwolle: Windesheim University of Applied Sciences, 2017).

Nikkie Gubbels and Rutger Kappe, *Stress and engagement. Exploratory study into the levels of stress and engagement among students of Inholland University of Applied Sciences* (in Dutch) (Amsterdam: Inholland University of Applied Sciences, 2017).

Ministry of Education, Culture, and Science, *Quality in Diversity. Strategic Agenda Higher Education and Research* (in Dutch) (The Hague: Ministry of Education, Culture, and Science, 2011).

Ministry of Education, Culture, and Science, *Selection and accessibility of higher education. Letter to Parliament* (in Dutch) (The Hague: Ministry of Education, Culture, and Science, 7 July 2017).

Royal Netherlands Academy of Arts and Sciences, *Dutch and/or English? Judicious choice of language in Dutch higher education* (in Dutch) (Amsterdam: Royal Netherlands Academy of Arts and Sciences, 2017).

Wilmar Schaufeli, Isabel Martinez, Alexandra Marquez Pinto, Marisa Salanova, and Arnold Bakker, 'Burnout and engagement in university students: A cross-national study', *Journal of Cross-Cultural Psychology*, 33(5) (2002): 464-481.

Setting the agenda: 'To whom are we answering'?[1]

Frank Miedema[2]

Until a few years ago it was still common, at least among academic scientists, for one to hear the viewpoint expressed that 'Science is essentially unpredictable and hence unplannable. The best thing to do therefore would be to give the scientist as much money as he wants to do what research he wants. Some of it would be bound to pay off, intellectually or economically or with luck both.' One might be forgiven for thinking that this quote comes from recent debates about open science or about directing publicly funded research on grand societal challenges. These lines are, however, from a book published in 1969 entitled *Science and Society* by Hilary Rose and Steven Rose. The authors point out that free research has traditionally been the perquisite of only a few, but for most academic scientists it has been at best an inspirational myth. For that minority, however, it is the rhetoric they use to protect their vested interests in the debate on how to decide what and whose research should be funded. This is a debate that remains controversial due to the intense and cut-throat competition for funding, while society realizes that science must be more responsible.

In the Netherlands, the National Health Council recently concluded that the dominant use of academic metrics had shaped the research agenda of the eight University Medical Centres in an undesirable way from the perspective of the public.[3] Fields of

---

1   This contribution is a slightly modified version of a blog post that appeared on BMJ Open: http://blogs.bmj.com/openscience/2018/01/24/setting-the-agenda-who-are-we-answering-to/.
2   The author is one of the founders of Science in Transition, a mission to reform the scientific system. See: http://scienceintransition.nl/en/about-science-in-transition.
3   See: https://www.gezondheidsraad.nl/en/task-and-procedure/areas-of-activity/innovatie-en-kennisinfrastructuur/research-that-makes-you-better.

research should be prioritized due to their connection to disease or economic and social burden were neglected over fields that are held in higher esteem from an academic perspective. Preventive medicine, public health research, chronic disease management, and rehabilitation medicine have lost to such areas as the genetics of psychiatric disorders and molecular cancer research. This is not related to excellence but due to goal displacement induced by a skewed system of incentives and rewards that are applied to allocate credit. How did we get to this point, and what can we do about it?

In recent decades, the evaluation of research, especially in the natural sciences and biomedical sciences, has become dominated by the use of metrics. This is an understandable response to the problem of increasing competition in a system that is rapidly growing. There was a need for quantitative criteria that could be used across a broad range of fields. Although they are poor proxies for quality, the metrics used include the number of papers published, the number of citations, the journal impact factor and the Hirsch Factor. This is increasingly being criticized. Indeed, these metrics favour basic research over fields of research that are closer to practical applications or that historically relied on other publication and citation practices. Due to strategic behaviour on the part of researchers, research that is socially and clinically the most relevant has suffered, while many young researchers are moving into already crowded fields that have done well in the metrics.

For an individual researcher, this makes perfect sense because researchers work in what can be described as a 'credibility cycle', where credit is 'the ability to actually do science' (Latour & Woolgar 1979). This means that, despite personal ideals and good intentions, in this incentive and reward system researchers find themselves pursuing not the work that would benefit public or preventive health or patient care the most but instead work that receives the most academic credit and is better for their career advancement. In this cycle of credibility, all actors — not only deans, department heads, group leaders, and PhD candidates

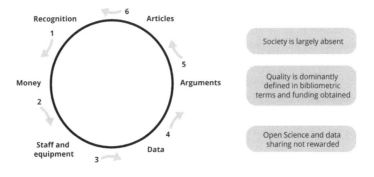

Adapted from Latour and Woolgar, 1979, Hessels et al, 2009

but also funders and journal editors — are each optimizing their interests, which are not in sync with the collective aims of science. One of the most striking consequences is that investments of time and effort in quality control such as peer reviews are not rewarded. This has led to the current situation where the global workforce of researchers annually produces about 1.5 million papers (in a still growing number of journals), many of which are of poor quality. It is now widely acknowledged that we have a serious reproducibility crisis in the biomedical and social sciences.

Is there a way to bring the credibility cycle in line with the original motivation of many researchers to contribute to improving the quality of life? One could argue that quality criteria related to the predicted technical, economic, or social impact of research on society are at least as important, and maybe even more important, than traditional markers of academic quality. But how are we to apply these fundamentally distinct criteria when evaluating science? How does this work in real-life decision-making at various levels? In the Netherlands, the National Health Council as well as the Ministry of Higher Education and Science have called for the development of a national science agenda and a shift in evaluation procedures towards societal impact. At the University Medical Center Utrecht, we are working on this shift

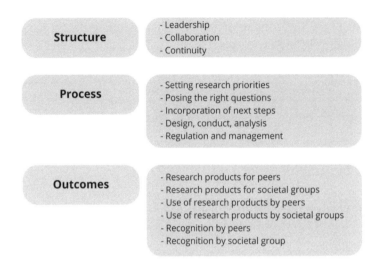

These are the main categories of the 'Indicators for impact' that are being used in evaluation pilots at University Medical Center Utrecht.

towards research evaluation based on societal impact. We have carried out pilot studies with a set of evaluation criteria that focus on processes and diverse outcomes that may include, in compliance with the concept of open science, data sets, biobanks, and biomaterials that are shared. Evaluation implies 'reading instead of counting' to appreciate the quality and impact of the research. In addition, we have invited representatives from non-academic societal stakeholders to sit on the expert review committees. Since researchers and staff were largely unfamiliar with these more labour-intensive evaluation practices, this was initially not met with only enthusiasm. Sarah de Rijcke of the Centre for Science and Technology Studies at Leiden University and her team are studying the reception of these interventions by different actors.

It is generally agreed that time is needed for a proper and fair quality assessment to evaluate our research in the light of the mission of University Medical Center Utrecht and the Faculty of Medicine to improve public health, cures and clinical care. In that light, it is very significant that Utrecht University decided to make long-term investments of millions of euros in interdisciplinary research hubs that, working together with societal stakeholders, aim to tackle key societal challenges. It all comes down to the question: To whom and what are we answering? Are we answering to patient and public needs or to internal academic criteria for excellence and career advancement? We must and can have both.

Bibliography

Bruno Latour and Steve Woolgar, *Laboratory Life: The Construction of Scientific Facts* (Princeton: Princeton University Press, 1979).

Hilary Rose and Steven Rose, *Science and Society* (London: Penguin, 1969).

Top: With about 150 other professors, Bert van der Zwaan bikes to a primary school in order to teach a class of ten to twelve-year-olds. Each professor visits a different group of children, and altogether over 100 primary schools participate. The classroom activities focus on research, the fun of science, and what it is like at a university. This highly successful annual event is called 'Meet the professor' and was started in 2016. Photo: Jos Kuklewski

Bottom: All professors participating in 'Meet the professor' are asked to make a selfie with their group of kids. This is Bert van der Zwaan's attempt. Photo: Bert van der Zwaan

Top: Bert van der Zwaan with Kurt Deketelaere, Secretary-General of the League of European Research Universities (LERU). In 2016, Bert van der Zwaan was appointed president of LERU. Photo: Steven Snoep

Bottom: Rectors (or Vice-Chancellors) of member universities of LERU meet in the University Hall in Utrecht. The portraits on the wall include those of Antonius Aemilius and Gisbertus Voetius, the second and third *Rectores* of Utrecht University in the first half of the seventeenth century. Van der Zwaan was Rector Magnificus number 333. Photo: Veerle van Kerckhove

Top: Bert van der Zwaan with the board of trustees of the Prince Claus Chair for Development and Equity and H.M. Queen Máxima of the Netherlands, who is honorary patron of the Prince Claus Chair. Utrecht University alternates with the International Institute of Social Studies of Erasmus University Rotterdam in appointing an outstanding young academic from a developing country to this chair. Photo: Robert Oosterbroek

Bottom: Bert van der Zwaan together with Jan van Zanen, mayor of the city of Utrecht, at a costumed parade to celebrate the university's anniversary. In 1836, during Utrecht University's bicentennial celebrations, the tone was set for this parade, which has since been organized by the fraternity *Utrechtsch Studenten Corps*. Photo: Bas van Hattum

Top: 'UIT' stands for Utrecht Introduction Time, a week in which the approximately 3,500 freshmen of Utrecht University are given information about the university, student life, the city, and about their study programme. Here, Bert van der Zwaan addresses the students. Photo: Robert Oosterbroek

Bottom: Bert van der Zwaan having a conversation with members of the board of one of the student organizations during drinks after the formal opening of the academic year in Utrecht's Dom Church. Photo: Robert Oosterbroek

On the need for universities to engage in lifelong learning

Joop Schippers

Even though economists have little reason to be very proud of the accomplishments of their discipline over the last decades, one economic concept that was developed already in the 1960s has stood the test of time, and that is the concept of human capital. Just as a firm needs physical capital such as buildings, machines, and raw materials to realize its production, human individuals can only be productive in the labour market if they have adequate knowledge and skills at their disposal. By investing time and money on education, people can enhance their human capital and become more productive. In addition to preferences for different types of work, innate ability determines how much each individual invests in her/his human capital. After entering the labour market, workers will acquire additional human capital in the form of experience and on-the-job learning. However, this is not the whole story. Existing human capital — just like the machines in the factory — is subject to wear and tear and consequently to depreciation. One of the explanatory factors is a person's ageing, which may result in a slower pace of pushing the buttons, less endurance, or what has come to be known as 'senior moments' ('I remember her face, but I cannot reproduce her name at this moment'). Another major factor is technological development. The higher the pace of technological innovation, the sooner individuals' knowledge and skills become obsolete and the higher the need for maintenance of existing knowledge and skills and investing in new forms of human capital. Some knowledge and skills depreciate more rapidly than others.

In the past, universities — as one of the major suppliers of human capital — could argue that a master's degree obtained at the age of 25, for example, would largely satisfy a career of 30 to 35 years. Some additional investment might be necessary (depending on the job, branch of industry, and discipline), but many alumni could do very well with their master's degree as 'a ticket to the labour market' that remained valid throughout their career. In recent years, two things have happened that challenge this validity. First, demographic challenges have obliged governments in several countries to raise the official retirement age in the future. One of the implications is that young people entering the labour market in their early twenties will have to be productive in that labour market for about half a century. Given the dynamics of the economy, this also implies that they will have to 'survive' more economic downturns, the risk of their employer going bankrupt, or the possibility that consumers will turn their attention to some other branch or product. Second, rapid technological innovation has increased the speed of depreciation of human capital, which in itself implies that the human capital acquired during one's initial education is less likely to be sufficient for a productive career than it used to be in the past.

So, if universities ever had the idea that they provided young people with a more or less 'complete' education —to use the language used when talking about human capital — this idea has rapidly become obsolete. Universities provide their students with enough knowledge and skills for a proper start in life and in the labour market — and this can be either at the bachelor's or the master's level — but from a life course perspective their job is not yet finished. Just as sustainable construction increasingly includes not only designing and realizing a building but also maintaining and finally dismantling the building, university education should not stop with a bachelor's or a master's degree but should also include maintenance in the form of post-initial learning opportunities. One could say that this is part of the social responsibility of the university. Then, of course, the question comes up how these post-initial learning opportunities should actually be shaped. The logical thing to do here seems to me to link the post-initial initiatives to the nature of the specific university. This way, all universities together (including those for applied sciences) can provide 'the market for lifelong learning' in higher education with a proper supply that matches all the needs, desires, and preferences of their potential 'customers'. To be more concrete, a university with a strong orientation towards teaching could develop a broad spectrum of courses that allow participants to become acquainted with recent developments in a particular discipline or regarding a specific topic.

For a research university, this approach may be less attractive from a what's-in-it-for-us perspective: even though teaching staff may find it refreshing to work with an older group of participants every now and then, for many professors it may also mean 'just another task' on top of all the other tasks that divert from their main goal in (professional) life — conducting (preferably ground-breaking) research. Therefore, research universities might prefer to link their post-initial educational initiatives more to their own already existing research activities. This probably implies a small-scale approach at a relatively high level. Consequently, from a strictly financial perspective, post-initial education is hardly likely to ever be a cash cow for typical research universities, while more teaching-oriented universities may find it an interesting source of additional financial means. Talking about financial means brings us back to the dismal science of economics. Who is going to pay for all these wonderful initiatives in the field of lifelong learning? Especially in an ever more flexible labour market, it is unlikely that either employers or individual workers would be willing to initiate major investments in lifelong learning. Both parties have strong incentives to wait until 'the other party moves'. So, without government interventions creating a proper institutional framework for lifelong learning and maybe some additional financial means (but that is not the most important government contribution; the major contribution is the break-through of the 'hold up' problem), there is a serious risk of too little investment in the maintenance and development of (new) human capital.

But if employers and individual workers are going to pay together, they will certainly demand that they have a proper say in what kind of activities universities are going to develop in the field of lifelong learning. So, contrary to bachelor's programmes that are primarily supply-driven (i.e., the university staff decides what knowledge and skills are relevant for students) and master's programmes that are partly supply-driven but also take into account students' labour market opportunities, lifelong learning programmes should be primarily demand-driven. This would push universities to engage in serious market research to take stock of societal and organizational needs, sometimes resulting in courses on topics relevant for a broad group of participants, sometimes resulting in specialized, in-company courses. Another strategy is to engage in more lasting and broader relations with a group of dedicated organizations. This strategy is especially suitable for research universities because they offer a broad spectrum of cooperation ranging from the use of organizational data to committed studies, joint research, and development activities, including activities primarily aimed at enlarging the knowledge and skills of the staff of the organizations. Set in a research context, activities in the field of lifelong learning may and should take the form of co-creation instead of a one-sided transfer of knowledge. Yes, indeed, the university's staff has much knowledge to offer, but the participants from the organizations are much more experienced when it comes to the utilization of this knowledge within an often multidisciplinary organizational context. So they are the ones who can challenge the learned scientists to descend from their ivory towers and check what their theories can accomplish in practice. Organized this way, lifelong learning will be fun for both scientists and participants. Instead of becoming a stand-alone activity fighting all usual bureaucratic fights within the university organization, it will develop into an integrated part of a traditional research university's core tasks.

Part 3

Reflections on learning and teaching

Diversifying the university menu

José van Dijck

In his engaging book on the future of higher education, Bert van der Zwaan argues his preference for a multiform and flexible system of higher education that can adapt to every future societal and academic challenge:

> In their vision of the future, universities should focus on having a diversity of forms, rather than striving for a uniformity that is grafted onto the Anglo-Saxon model. (...) In the diverse university system of the future, there must be room for each university to develop its own individual profile, leading to the emergence of a multiform and flexible system that is able to adapt to almost every change. (Van der Zwaan 2017: 243).

If universities want to survive the next 25 years, they should diversify their menus and offer a mix of proven and experimental approaches to teaching and research. We are currently training students for future jobs that, to a large extent, do not even exist today, many current jobs will be taken over by self-learning intelligent machines, and new jobs may require a range of skills that we cannot even imagine right now. Diversifying the education ecosystem is indeed an important precondition to train workers to keep training themselves. So what mixture of old and new forms can universities offer to prepare the next generation of knowledge workers?

We can already witness today how technology companies are increasingly taking over parts of the learning trajectory from schools and universities; digital courses and online training programmes often serve to select the brightest minds from the sea of talents. Universities will likely no longer have a patent on learning and credentialing systems, as alternative credentialing mechanisms will arise to assess and accredit the skills that people acquire along the way. Where campuses once used to be the place for scouting young talents, tech campuses (mostly in Silicon Valley) have themselves turned into places of continuous learning. In the campus model of the future, there will be a coming and going of students, employees, faculty, and personnel in high-density brainports. University campuses may still be the primary playground for young adults, and yet these campuses will increasingly also cater to learners of all ages and all levels of experience. If switching careers two or three times during a professional lifetime becomes the new norm, universities need to be adapting rapidly to new contingents of learners. Some tech executives dream of a future university campus where students each follow their own personalized learning trajectory, buoyed by their own digital personal assistants. It is easy to fantasize how, by the year 2030, each student will have his or her own AI tutor and mentor — an app-voice not unlike Samantha's in Spike Jonze's 2013 movie *Her* who personalizes each student's learning experience. Such an encouraging AI assistant may be equipped to review Statistics 101 assignments while also engaging in dialogues to test a student's understanding of Plato's *Republic*. A scenario in which the 'automated' part of learning is taken over by algorithms and the basic part of teaching is taken over by programmers may be regarded as a welcome reduction of teachers' workload to some, while others think it signals the beginning of the displacement of teachers. In whatever form, personalized digital environments are going to be part of the university's offerings in 2040, if only because large numbers of working professionals are in need of constant training upgrades.

Indeed, the diversification of education does not mean that the university should give up on its proven methods of learning. On the contrary, the old-style monologue lecture by the erudite teacher in front of 200 students will still be part of the menu some 22 years from now. Just as theatre was never replaced by film or television, students can still learn from the eloquent professor mesmerizing an audience with her voice. One thing that should never disappear from a student's diet is the opportunity to engage in the social activity of learning with their peers. In a world that is inundated with data and information, interpretation and rational arguments are more important than ever. And the best contexts in which to learn such skills are small college classes where students are not just beneficiaries of expert knowledge shared by their teachers but where they also acquire the necessary social skills to engage in dialogue with each other. As much as digital tutoring can help students become better learners, education is fundamentally a social activity where students and teachers need to interact.

Much has been said about the need for students to become experts in one specific discipline or one type of knowledge; at the same time, though, they need to be trained more generally in various subject areas. So universities need to offer both highly specialized education and broader training. The so-called T-shaped professional will be the best insurance for future employability. Ideally, the expertise and skills a student acquires in college would be transferable to other applications in the workforce. The ability to adapt easily to new areas of expertise is something students need to learn at universities. Therefore, it is important to pair off disciplinary training with interdisciplinary learning and dialogue. Over the past ten years, professors have increasingly become engaged in cross-disciplinary research projects. Exposing students to, and engaging them in, such efforts will prove crucial to strengthening students' adaptability. Collaborations across disciplines not only prepare students for future professions, they also help them become better problem-solvers.

Finally, let us reflect a little longer on the most crucial asset that makes most university-based curricula still relevant and valuable today: an emphasis on *Bildung* and on basic academic skills such as critical, independent thinking and analytical acuity. To start with the former, the best colleges have always prided themselves in offering a coherent curriculum: not just a dinner table filled with appetizers, entrees, and desserts but a carefully timed meal with the right amounts of knowledge offered at the right time in the right order. *Bildung* and digital environments are not necessarily rivalling goods, but it is certainly true that while the former has always been firmly curriculum-based, the latter thrives on the contingency of de-bundling courses from curricula and decoupling assignments and degrees from institutions. Taking in bits and pieces from a personalized menu seems so much more efficient than waiting out a formal dinner at a perfectly set dinner table. And yet it is important to realize why the latter has been so valuable and effective as an educational experience for many centuries. Perhaps the most crucial ingredient of any future university education will be students' ability to think independently paired off with a curiosity-driven mind-set and a tolerance towards considering new insights and knowledge. Each and every part of a student's education should centre on his or her abilities to raise questions, to articulate what kind of knowledge is needed to solve a problem, and to leverage this knowledge without pandering to special interests. There is not one single module or course that can train students to adopt such an academic attitude; instead, it is the primary task of a university to instil an appetite for independent and analytical thinking in every single student's brain during every minute of their education. Training students in *how to acquire* valuable knowledge, even as the *type* of knowledge they acquire will certainly change over time, may be the best investment in future wisdom. Whereas knowledge ages, wisdom prepares for rejuvenation.

While there is no ultimate recipe for the best university in 2040, the strategy to offer a diverse and balanced meal to students may be our best bet: keeping all-time favourites while adding the most promising of new flavours. One thing the university of 2040 cannot do without is a rector who can act like a visionary chef: a leader who simply knows when to embrace innovations and when to take them with a grain of salt. It is too bad that Bert van der Zwaan has to leave the kitchen when we need him most!

Bibliography

Bert van der Zwaan, *Higher Education in 2040 — A Global Approach* (Amsterdam: Amsterdam University Press, 2017).

The importance of evidence-based development of teaching and learning at university

Sari Lindblom and Jukka Kola

Universities will be faced with many challenges in the future. A significant increase in participation in higher education (Van der Zwaan 2017) has made the student population more and more diverse (Guri-Rosenblit, Šebková & Teichler 2007). The universities receive 'criticism from the outside world' (Van der Zwaan 2017: 5) because of the mass nature of education, the focus on efficiency and research output, and the lack of collaboration with industry. At the same time, competition in the higher-education sector has intensified, which makes the landscape of educational offerings for students ever more complex and difficult to judge in terms of quality. In this fast-changing higher education context, the evidence-based development of degree programmes becomes more and more relevant. The evidence-based discipline-specific development of teaching and learning is a key principle at the University of Helsinki, implemented to enhance the quality of students' learning outcomes. Learning and teaching processes take place in real-life environments and are therefore very complicated in nature. Research can help identify factors that contribute to high-quality teaching and learning (see, for example, Gibbs 2017; Stensaker, Bilbow, Breslow & Van der Vaart 2017). Some findings from educational research often make sense intuitively and can even sound self-evident, but it is important, particularly in research-intensive universities, to generate empirical evidence to confirm teachers' instincts (Lindblom-Ylänne & Breslow 2017). For example, systematic evidence has demonstrated that intrinsic study motivation, personal interest in studying, and self-regulation skills are related to study success at university (e.g. Entwistle 2009; Pintrich 2004).

However, the development of teaching and learning cannot be based on previous experiences or on intuition only, as the empirical evidence often reveals complicated inter-relationships or even counter-intuitive aspects that need to be taken into account (Lindblom-Ylänne and Breslow 2017). For example, working while studying at university can both enhance and impede study progress and success depending on how skilful students are at organized studying and effort management and in self-regulating their study processes (see Tuononen, Parpala, Mattsson & Lindblom-Ylänne 2016). Research on university-level learning and teaching can very seldom give simple and straightforward answers because these phenomena are so complex in nature, but it is nonetheless necessary to systematically carry on collecting empirical evidence on the teaching and learning processes in different disciplines to find effective and functional study and teaching methods for each study programme (Lindblom-Ylänne & Breslow 2017). A strong research-teaching nexus is also important in order to ensure the high quality of students' learning outcomes. Although in research-intensive universities, academics perceive the link between research and teaching as positive (e.g. Elen, Lindblom-Ylänne & Clement 2007), we lack systematic evidence on a beneficial link between active involvement in research and the quality of teaching and students' learning outcomes (Hattie & Marsh 1996; Verburgh, Elen & Lindblom-Ylänne 2007). Engaging students in research and research-like activities can bridge the gap between teaching and research.

The University of Helsinki has undergone a substantial curriculum-reform process during which all bachelor's and master's programmes were redesigned on the basis of the following generally agreed main principles: (1) The creation of broad multidisciplinary bachelor's programmes followed by more focused and specialised master's programmes; (2) The enhancement of the employability of graduates by adding compulsory, discipline-specific course modules on working-life skills and competences and by increasing cooperation between the university and working life; (3) Clearly and concretely defined learning outcomes in all courses of all programmes so that students are aware of what they are expected to learn, how their learning will be assessed, and how they should monitor their own progress; (4) The creation of shared degree structures, which enables the planning of individual study paths and the selection of course modules from different disciplines.

From the beginning of the academic year 2017-2018, the University of Helsinki launched 32 multidisciplinary bachelor's programmes. The total number of bachelor's programmes was reduced to one-third to better serve the students and to enhance collaboration among teachers representing different disciplines. The 60 new master's programmes are more specialised. Of these, 35 are international. The Centre for University Teaching and Learning supports the evidence-based, discipline-specific development of teaching and learning in the new degree programmes by allocating pedagogical support for teachers to develop new teaching methods and to monitor students' progress and the quality of their learning outcomes. In addition, the Teachers' Academy is a network of distinguished teachers who have key roles in their own disciplines in emphasising the importance of high-quality teaching in the research-intensive atmosphere at the University of Helsinki. The academic staff of the Centre for Teaching and Learning collaborates actively with the Teachers' Academy, and together they form a task force to enhance the scholarship of teaching and learning at university (e.g. Hutchings & Shulman 1999; Kreber 2013; Trigwell, Martin, Benjamin & Prosser 2000).

Interestingly, the design principles described above are very much aligned with key points listed by Bert van der Zwaan in 'The curriculum of the Future', the last chapter of his book *Higher Education in 2040* (2017). Van der Zwaan also emphasises the importance of collaboration between different disciplines. Offering more interdisciplinary programmes at universities is essential to prepare students to work in multidisciplinary teams in working life. The University of Helsinki also supports the arrangement where teachers work in teams in which the teachers represent various disciplines instead of the traditional model where one teacher teaches one course. This broadens students' worldviews and their understanding of the phenomena under study. According to Van der Zwaan (2017: 228), too little attention has been paid to the labour market and to the societal impact of university education: '[W]hen we bear in mind that university curricula tend to be supply-driven, that is, driven by academic traditions or lecturers' interests; research universities in particular are not demand-driven in the sense that they respond to demand from society.' At the University of Helsinki, the new degree programmes emphasise working-life relevance and the learning of working-life competences systematically from the beginning of a student's university studies. We agree with Van der Zwaan that research skills, such as designing appropriate research and using the right methods, as well as academic thinking skills, such as critical evaluation, need to be given priority in addition to disciplinary knowledge. Because universities educate academic experts for an unknown future, it is important that students develop academic skills that can be flexibly tailored and modified to the changing needs of working life.

Van der Zwaan writes about a shift from curriculum-based education to personalized, customised education. This has also been an objective of the recent curriculum reform at the University of Helsinki. The possibility to tailor degrees to meet students' personal interests and the opportunity to follow individual study paths inside the curricula help students to engage in their studies and support smooth study progress and the completion of degrees. Van der Zwaan further predicts a decrease in campus-based teaching in favour of online education. Even though the University of Helsinki aims to digitalize the teaching and learning processes, this will be accomplished by integrating face-to-face education with digital solutions. We consider digitalization as a tool to enhance quality, not a goal in itself. In addition, digitalisation provides students and teachers with more flexibility to organise learning and teaching without losing the important face-to-face interaction. Finally, Van der Zwaan foresees that university education will become more and more modular in nature as the demand for lifelong learning increases. According to him, 'modularisation enables each student to select individually those parts of the curriculum in which he or she is interested' (2017: 234). We argue that it is important to separate studying for a degree from continuing education. In further and continuing education, it is possible to concentrate on selecting modules based on one's own motivation and interest. However, when students are studying for a bachelor's or master's degree, it is not possible to only select courses on the basis of personal interests. Different courses of the study programmes complement each other, and as studies in specific programmes proceed, students' expertise of the discipline will gradually deepen and broaden. This guarantees that graduates can successfully work as competent academic experts in different areas of society.

Bibliography

Jan Elen, Sari Lindblom-Ylänne, and Mieke Clement, 'Faculty development in research-intensive universities: The role of academics' conceptions on the relationship between research and teaching', *International Journal for Academic Development*, 12 (2) (2007), pp. 123-139.

Graham Gibbs, 'Reflections', in Björn Stensaker, Grahame Bilbow, Lori Breslow and Rob van der Vaart (eds), *Strengthening teaching and learning in research universities: Strategies and initiatives for institutional change* (London: Palgrave Macmillan, 2017), pp. 215-224.

Sarah Guri-Rosenblit, Helena Šebková, and Ulrich Teichler, 'Massification and diversity of higher education systems: Interplay of complex dimensions', *Higher Education Policy*, 20 (2007), pp. 373-389.

John Hattie and Herbert W. Marsh, 'The relationship between research and teaching: A meta-analysis', *Review of Educational Research*, 66 (1996), pp. 507-542.

Pat Hutchings and Lee Shulman, 'The scholarship of teaching: New elaborations, new developments', *Change: The Magazine of Higher Learning*, 31(5) (1999), pp. 10-15.

Carolin Kreber, 'Empowering the scholarship of teaching: An Arendtian and critical perspective', *Studies in Higher Education* 38(6) (2013), pp. 857-869.

Sari Lindblom-Ylänne and Lori Breslow, 'The importance of evidence-based enhancement of the quality of learning and teaching in research-intensive universities', in Björn Stensaker, Grahame Bilbow, Lori Breslow, and Rob van der Vaart (eds), *Strengthening teaching and learning in research universities: Strategies and initiatives for institutional change*. (London: Palgrave Macmillan, 2017), pp. 187-213.

Björn Stensaker, Grahame Bilbow, Lori Breslow, and Rob van der Vaart (eds), *Strengthening teaching and learning in research universities: Strategies and initiatives for institutional change* (London: Palgrave Macmillan, 2017).

Tarja Tuononen, Anna Parpala, Markus Mattsson, and Sari Lindblom-Ylänne, 'Work experience in relation to study pace and thesis grade: Investigating the mediating role of student learning', *Higher Education*, 72(1) (2016), pp. 41-58.

Keith Trigwell, Elaine Martin, Joan Benjamin, and Michael Prosser, 'Scholarship of teaching: A model', *Higher Education Research & Development*, 19 (2) (2000), pp. 155-168.

An Verburgh, Jan Elen, and Sari Lindblom-Ylänne, 'Investigating the myth of the positive relationship between teaching and research in higher education: A review on the empirical research', *Studies in Philosophy and Education*, 26(5) (2007), pp. 449-465.

Bert van der Zwaan, *Higher Education in 2040 — A Global Approach* (Amsterdam: Amsterdam University Press, 2017).

Re-thinking the higher education curriculum: Challenges, possibilities, and dreams

Dilly Fung

How full of possibilities higher education is today, and yet how difficult it can be for the sector to engage powerfully with the modern world. News of local and international changes and challenges — social, cultural, technological, ecological, professional, political, and economic — confronts us hour by hour. In any given moment, we see another news item, a picture, a tweet, the publication of yet another article; they appear unannounced, fighting for our attention. We hear the voices of the economically privileged cut across one another, polyphonic and unresolved, while other voices are silenced. Arguments about what is 'fake' and what is 'true' swarm through the airwaves. In the meantime, communities worldwide are in need, sometimes in desperate need, of solutions to their challenges.

My dream, and that of many, is of scholarship that helps individuals and communities cut through the morass of (mis) information and that sets us on an evidence-based path that leads to an increase in 'the global common good' (UNESCO 2015). Yet in the crossfire of populism, perpetually changing policies, and the press, that dream seems to be tantalizingly out of reach. How can the higher education sector respond more effectively to contemporary society, in all its kaleidoscopic intensity? More than that, how can it lead the way to a better future? If the impact of higher education on today's world is to be even greater, we need to re-think student education and its relationship to research. The sector drew traditionally on the Humboldtian principle of the unity of research and teaching, but in higher education institutions across the world the lived experience of scholars is of two areas of activity not united but divided.

Tackling this division is certainly a challenge. Funding streams, national policies, and institutional structures and processes all forge divisions between the practices of research and student education. These divisions are underpinned by a difference in markers of esteem and reward for those who commit to these two areas; senior prizes and promotions are still orientated predominantly towards research success, with excellence in teaching or educational leadership seen as less prestigious. Education-related activity is even seen as simply administrative or managerial and not academic work (Fung & Gordon 2016), when in fact education (teaching and education-focused leadership) should surely be viewed, as Boyer argued (Boyer 1990), as an area of scholarship that is of equal importance to research and deeply interconnected with it. In addition, we often research and teach from our disciplinary islands, and here is a key area of disconnect between student education and research. Increasingly research is interdisciplinary, addressing complex global challenges using multiple analytical lenses and methodologies, yet students too often study in a narrow field. Alternatively, they study in a range of fields but are not asked explicitly to make critical and creative intellectual connections between those fields, even though challenging them to do so would help prepare them for the multifaceted challenges that lie ahead in the workplace and in life. Another key challenge is that of the distance between higher education institutions and their local and wider communities. Our institutions undertake vital research, and this research provides intellectual arguments, artistic contributions, technological solutions, and professional developments; without these, our communities would be much the poorer. But for many citizens, locally and globally, research is hidden. It is a mystery, mediated perhaps by brief and potentially misleading media reports of the latest developments.

In a recent monograph (Fung 2017), I argue that it is possible to create better synergies between the research undertaken by universities and students' learning by adopting a Connected Curriculum. We *can* take a series of practical steps that build on the excellent research already underway, enhance the quality of student education, and in doing so increase the impact that higher education has on society. And we can do all this through a joined-up approach that is values-based, directed specifically at making an even greater contribution to good in the world. When designing taught degree programmes, we have traditionally started with a fixed body of knowledge in a particular discipline or field. We have shaped courses around content and then thought about how students can acquire that knowledge. It was as if faculty members held a number of pre-defined items in a mental suitcase, and it was the work of the students to end up with a reasonably similar suitcase full of comparable items of knowledge. Students who were particularly skilled at recalling ideas and facts in timed examinations did well in their degree programmes. In turn, some were to become faculty members of the future, and set out to hand the same suitcase full of knowledge on to the next generation. But instead of thinking of curriculum as primarily a fixed body of content to be taught, we need to see it as all of the learning opportunities and methods available to students today as they study for their degree awards. We can create a series of learning opportunities that are research-rich (Fung, Besters-Dilger & Van der Vaart 2017), engaging students much more richly with research — with its questions and practices as well as with its findings. And this means empowering students to learn though active enquiry and investigation at every level of study, so that they develop vital critical, ethical, and practical skills along with the confidence to apply these in unforeseen contexts.

How in practice can we do this? In our digital world, the possibilities are far more numerous and diverse than they were traditionally. In any given moment, a student can access a range of sources and resources that would have been beyond our imaginings a generation ago. Students can speak to others in real time across national boundaries; they can collaborate in

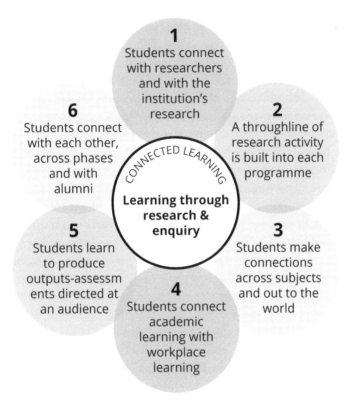

Fung 2017

person or virtually with others who may have quite different skill sets and perspectives. In addition, students can become producers or creators of new communications. One key dimension of the Connected Curriculum framework (see figure) is the use of outward-facing student assessments. This involves assessing student learning through 'real world' communications directed at specified audiences. The forms of these communications can vary: examples include articles, podcasts, video documentaries, blogs, reports, multi-media presentations, and policy papers, but the possibilities are many. The joy here is that where students are engaging actively in research and enquiry, and where in doing so they are coming to understand the latest research produced by their institutions, they can also communicate the excellence and the findings of that research to their communities. They are able, through a series of collaborations with peers and with more senior scholars in their institutions, to communicate scholarship to the public and even to draw the public into the research sphere to become participants and partners. They can work towards a curated portfolio of outputs in various forms that showcases the best of what they have achieved, telling the story of their investigations, their arguments, their skills, and their values.

How might these dreams be characterized? The first dream entails bringing our diverse, international students into what Angela Brew (2006) calls 'an inclusive scholarly community'. A combination of research-rich learning opportunities and outward-facing student assessments prepares each student for change — changes in the workplace, in society, and in their own careers. But it also promotes collaboration, peer-engagement, mutual respect, and a strong sense of shared endeavour, all of which are so greatly needed in our divisive age. The second is to empower all students, whatever their background, to develop a strong and confident voice. By learning richly through active enquiry from the beginning to the end of their degree programmes, students engage critically with the kaleidoscope of pictures and voices that surround them and confront the importance and limitations of evidence and 'truth'. In doing so, they not only acquire the knowledge, understandings, and skilful practices they need for the future, they also explore and develop their own identities, places, and voices in the academy, in the professions, and in the world. The final dream is that through the artful design of a menu of active learning and assessment activities, we forge stronger connections between higher education and communities. Through the creation of outward-facing communications artefacts directed at real-world audiences, all scholars (students, teachers, professionals, and researchers) develop stronger and more confident voices; they also learn to listen more, paying even greater attention to local and global perspectives and becoming even more responsive to community needs and challenges. The voices of all scholars, including those traditionally silenced, enrich contemporary debate even more loudly and clearly, contributing to a better future for us all.

Bibliography

Ernest L. Boyer, *Scholarship reconsidered: Priorities of the professoriate* (Princeton: Carnegie Foundation for the Advancement of Teaching, 1990).

Angela Brew, *Research and teaching: Beyond the divide* (London: Palgrave Macmillan, 2006).

Dilly Fung, *A Connected Curriculum for Higher Education* (London: UCL Press, 2017). http://discovery.ucl.ac.uk/1558776/1/A-Connected-Curriculum-for-Higher-Education.pdf

Dilly Fung, Juliane Besters-Dilger, and Rob van der Vaart, *Excellent education in research-rich universities. Position Paper* (Brussels: League of European Research Universities, 2017).

Dilly Fung and Claire Gordon, *Rewarding educators and education leaders in research-intensive universities* (York: Higher Education Academy, 2016). https://www.heacademy.ac.uk/sites/default/files/rewarding_educators_and_education_leaders.pdf

UNESCO, *Rethinking Education: Towards a Global Common Good?* (Paris: United Nations Educational, Scientific and Cultural Organization, 2015). http://unesdoc.unesco.org/images/0023/002325/232555e.pdf

The university as a community in the digital age

Anka Mulder

In *Higher Education in 2040 – A Global Approach*, Bert van der Zwaan states that there are many definitions of universities and that '*The* university does not exist' (31). I agree and picked one from the Internet: on Wikipedia, a university is defined as 'an institution of higher (tertiary) education which awards academic degrees in various disciplines. Universities typically provide undergraduate and postgraduate education.' This is quite a matter-of-fact definition. Wikipedia also states that 'the word "university" is derived from the Latin *universitas magistrorum et scholarium*, which roughly means "community of teachers and scholars"'.[1] I believe that the word 'community' is vital in this definition and that its importance is often underestimated in higher education. Bert van der Zwaan describes digitalization as one of the megatrends that will affect higher education institutions. In this essay, I will elaborate on this and give an overview of how information technology influences higher education in logistics and administration, in how we teach, what we teach, and what digitalization means for the higher education system.[2] I will conclude with the part that is often overlooked: what digitalization can mean for the university as a community.

The effects of digitalization are clear in the *logistics and administration* of higher education. It is almost impossible to imagine student registration, classroom and timetable planning, or tuition administration without digital means. In our back offices, IT has been around for many years. It has helped universities to become more efficient and effective. More recent

---

1   https://en.wikipedia.org/wiki/University.
2   For a more detailed overview, see Mulder 2017.

are developments in the process of teaching, i.e. in *how we teach*. Online publication of higher education content through, for example, Open Course Ware and Massive Open Online Courses (MOOCs) have made more content more easily accessible to many. And even if MOOCs have been criticized for mostly attracting learners who already hold a degree, it is a fact that millions of learners worldwide have used courses on online platforms such as EdX, Coursera, and Future Learn. The availability of online materials has also created new didactic possibilities such as flipped classroom teaching. Other developments include gaming in education and the emergence of learning analytics. Learning analytics have been around for a while, but the new generation of learning management systems provide many more opportunities to improve and customize education. As they enable universities to generate and analyse vast amounts of educational data, they will help staff to study how individual students learn, what they already know, understand, et cetera. In that sense, learning analytics will help universities to provide more personalized and evidence-based education.

Digitalization will also affect *what we teach*. It is clear that digital skills and knowledge will be needed in almost every job in the future. Whether our graduates will become teachers, medical doctors, architects, or financial specialists, they will need to know how to use digital means in their professions. However, many workers are not prepared for the digital work environment (OECD 2016). And a thorough understanding of the digital world is necessary to prepare our students not only for a career but also as citizens who understand the world around them and who can critically reflect on the possibilities and dangers that digitalization offers. It is clear that universities have a role in this.

Finally, digitalization will affect the *higher education system*. If there is one particular point that has been discussed extensively in the last ten years, it is this: what is the effect of IT on the higher education system, and will we as a sector still exist ten or twenty years from now? The most famous contribution to this discussion was perhaps that of Harvard Professor Clayton Christensen. Christensen describes how developments in IT as a disruptive technology have revolutionized encyclopaedias and the music, video, and photography industries. He believes this will also happen in higher education. Throughout history, universities have had no serious competition from outside their sector, but the emergence of online possibilities has created disruptive, for-profit competitors who can offer education at a lower price. It is easy to see what this could mean: many higher education institutions, notably those with high tuition fees and mediocre education — i.e. low value for money — will face serious competition from the private sector and face a shortened life expectancy. If universities do not adapt, they risk having their own Encyclopaedia Britannica or Kodak 'moment'. Universities have to find innovative, less expensive ways to carry out higher education (see Christensen & Eyring 2011).

So much for the threats to the sector. Digitalization holds opportunities as well. Universities can showcase their top teachers and top educational materials online and improve their visibility worldwide. It also makes it easier to cooperate nationally and internationally and innovate education with partner universities. Digitalization enables universities to expand their educational portfolio efficiently by sharing online courses with partner universities and including those of their partner institutions in their own programmes for credit, like nine top 100 universities did when they set up the Global Virtual Exchange Alliance in 2017.[3]

As I mentioned, the word 'community' in the definition of universities usually receives little attention. Universities and higher education are often described fully from the perspective of the curriculum. But students do not only come to university to study chemistry or philosophy, or to become a good industrial designer or civil engineer. They also attend university because of the community or the social place it is. Higher education institutions are not only places where students participate in a curriculum. They are also meeting places where students grow up, make friends, develop a network for life, and may even find their future partner. IT has had a major impact on what 'community' or 'social' means in many sectors. Billions of us use Facebook, LinkedIn, or Whatsapp to communicate with family, personal, or business contacts. Big software agents have changed industries such as the taxi, hotel, and tourism sectors by acting as a social medium or broker between people and products. So far, these brokers have had limited effect on higher education. Even the main MOOC platforms, EdX and Coursera, offer only limited 'social higher education media' possibilities beyond the curriculum. Universities themselves have not been active in this respect either. It is not as if there are no possibilities. On the contrary, there are plenty: connecting potential students with universities, for example, or graduates with employers, students with alumni, students who struggle with a course with those who can help, perhaps even connecting likeminded students for potential friendship and beyond.

Interestingly, higher education institutions' role in 'real life' is growing as they have become much more permeable, open not only to students and academics but also to companies, start-ups, and with the cities and regions in which they are located through

---

3   See: https://www.tudelft.nl/en/2017/tu-delft/international-universities-celebrate-signing-the-agreement-for-virtual-exchange/.

community engagement programmes. This means that their 'community' role has become stronger. It seems only logical that they do not only open up in 'real life' but also online. They have the connections and the data, and with that the possibility to play their 'community' and 'social' role online as well. If they choose not to, then corporate data brokers such as LinkedIn, Facebook, or HotCourses will surely do so. Van der Zwaan describes digitalization as a megatrend that will have a major impact on higher education but not as one that will threaten the existence of the system: campus education will still be around in 2040. Although predicting the future can be as unreliable as gazing into a crystal ball, it is important that we have thought through a range of possible scenarios. But whatever happens, if we want the higher education institution to succeed in the digital age, we will need to include digitalization in what we teach and use it to innovate, improve quality, and become more efficient. Most of all, we have to use its potential to increase our 'community' role.

Bibliography

C.M. Christensen and H.J. Eyring, *The Innovative University: Changing the DNA of Higher Education from the Inside Out* (New York: Wiley, 2011).

Anka Mulder, *Dutch universities and technology in education* (in Dutch) (Delft: TU Delft, 2017). See: https://ankamulder.weblog.tudelft.nl/files/2017/08/Nederlandse-universiteiten-en-technologie-in-onderwijs-Anka-Mulder-Printversie.pdf

OECD, 'Skills for a digital world', *Policy Brief on the Future of Work,* December 2016, pp. 1-4.

Bert van der Zwaan, *Higher Education in 2040 — A Global Approach* (Amsterdam: Amsterdam University Press, 2017).

Part 4

Reflections on the global and the local

Building the first global network university

John Sexton

I am delighted to write in honour of Bert van der Zwaan, whose seminal book *Higher Education in 2040 — A Global Approach* has influenced an entire generation of leaders in higher education. This essay provides just one example of how New York University has embraced Rector van der Zwaan's concepts of global higher education.

In 2006, leadership teams in Abu Dhabi and New York University set ambitious goals as they conceptualized the partnership that created NYU Abu Dhabi. They hoped to attract academic leaders and students who were as outstanding as those at the world's finest universities. A decade later, even those expectations would prove modest compared to what has happened. From the beginning, NYU Abu Dhabi was envisioned as a research university, with all that implies, into which a liberal arts college would be fully integrated. Beginning in 2007, three years before the first freshman would arrive, the team set out to recruit faculty members. Some would circulate periodically from among existing faculty at NYU New York. Others would be selected by the departments or units in New York specifically to be in Abu Dhabi most of the time. Together, they would develop the liberal arts curriculum of the new campus. That same year, some of NYU's lead faculty began research projects in Abu Dhabi that operated jointly with work being conducted in New York. And faculty members began to call leading experts from around the globe to conferences in Abu Dhabi — several dozen each year — that spanned the disciplines.

The initial team leader was one of New York's leading deans, who moved to Abu Dhabi with her husband and young children. The successful president of one of America's leading liberal arts colleges left that college to become the inaugural vice chancellor of NYU Abu Dhabi. A leader of a major initiative in genomics in New York moved with his family to Abu Dhabi, co-locating his lab, to be the campus provost, even as a new genomics building and faculty hiring initiative had begun in New York. And so on, from admissions to public safety to student life to technology, many of the very best faculty and staff joined the project with enthusiasm. Those who chose to join NYUAD had different motivations. Some of NYU's leading faculty were drawn by the mission and the opportunity to build a curriculum, such as the innovative science curriculum that was unencumbered by the obstacles associated with reforming an existing structure. Others were attracted by research interests, as was the case with a Middle Eastern Studies professor whose hope, now realized, was to organize definitive translations of major Arabic language works, or the linguistic neuroscientist who was interested in the languages of the region. By September 2010, when the first undergraduates arrived, there was already a well-established culture of advanced academic research, while faculty teams committed to teaching and mentoring the incoming class had implemented the foundations of the new curriculum.

Not surprisingly, the groundbreaking undergraduate opportunity in Abu Dhabi appealed to a high-talent group of students. The admissions team sought a cohort of students — literally from around the globe — who were 'clearly admissible, on the traditional norms, to ANY college or university in the world'. But, from the start, the admissions team understood that finding students who met this traditional standard alone would not be enough. Each admitted student had to manifest a 'cosmopolitan gene' that revealed a commitment to creating a global community that relished diversity. The NYU Abu Dhabi admissions process occurs in two stages. The first stage is similar to the standard processes at most top schools: an assessment of a file of academic achievements and standardized tests. In this first stage, the team assesses the candidate on traditional criteria and makes a judgment call about the applicant's commitment to ecumenical values. From this assessment, a set of 'finalists' (about five per cent of all applicants) is created; these finalists are then brought to Abu Dhabi for a two-day Candidates' Weekend — the second stage — consisting of interviews, classes, written exercises, and other tests. After this latter assessment, where the staff evaluates not only intellectual talent but also the commitment to the values of the enterprise, a decision is made whether to offer admissions. About half of the students who come to the Candidates' Weekend receive offers.

The goal in the first year was to open with 100 such students. Since the most successful liberal arts colleges in the United States enjoyed a 60 per cent yield on their offers of admission — that is, 60 per cent of those applicants who were offered a spot in the class chose to attend — the team sought 180 candidates worthy of offers. From that very first year, the results were validating. Just two per cent of the applicants for the inaugural class of undergraduates at NYU Abu Dhabi were offered admission — fewer than 200 out of over 9,000 applicants. The students came from 39 countries and spoke 43 languages. Nearly 90 per cent were at least bilingual. Their SAT verbal scores stood at 770 at the class's 75th percentile, and their math scores were at 780 at the 75th percentile — scores matching the most highly selective universities in the world. A remarkable 79 per cent who were offered spots in the class accepted, a much higher percentage than even the most selective liberal arts colleges in the United States and possibly a higher percentage than any other major university. The accepted students declined offers from eight of the ten top liberal arts universities in the United States and eighteen of the top 25 research universities. In its very first year, NYU Abu Dhabi established itself as one of the world's most selective undergraduate colleges and, arguably, the first truly international university.

Apart from the attraction of Abu Dhabi itself and its connection to the global network structure, NYU Abu Dhabi offered students a unique education. The initial student-faculty ratio was three to one, and the ratio will never exceed eight to one. The curriculum was strong, involving a tutorial form of education that completely integrates opportunities to participate in advanced research with a strong liberal arts core. The faculty was stellar, including some of the top professors from NYU New York and leading educators who have been deans, department chairs, and chaired professors from other top universities. And every researcher was committed to mentoring undergraduates. Still, as attractive as Abu Dhabi and the opportunities for learning there may have been to this initial cohort, the key factor in their choice of NYU Abu Dhabi was the prospect of working with others who share a cosmopolitan (in Appiah's sense) view of the world — not only in Abu Dhabi but on the other campuses of the global network university. For all the advantages of NYU Abu Dhabi, if it were a traditional university rather than a portal in a global network university, it would not have appealed to these students. The actual experience of this first cohort of NYU Abu Dhabi students confirmed the judgment made by this group of pioneers: over the four years, all but two of that first class spent at least a full semester studying away; the average student visited ten countries as part of an academic experience; 85 per cent of them held internships; 70 per cent did community service; and over a third had academic work published. Meanwhile, the NYU Abu Dhabi class and faculty have expanded, but the quality of that first group of arrivals has been maintained. In fact, by the customary indicators, the quality of each succeeding class has increased. The faculty has compiled a record of research productivity of the highest standards. And the careful work of the admissions team is now manifesting in four sets of graduates whose achievements are staggering. With fewer than 1,500 graduates in these classes, there are ten Rhodes Scholars. More remarkably, nearly all students who entered in the fall of 2010 graduated in the spring of 2014. Students who had come from every corner of the world stayed right through the four years, thrived, and left with a love for their college and Abu Dhabi.

The immediate success of NYU Abu Dhabi, even in its early stages, drew the attention of the leadership of China, both at the national and local level in Shanghai and Pudong. Based on their scan of major innovations in higher education, they approached NYU with the proposal that the university establish a full portal campus in Shanghai's Pudong District. The university, seeing an exciting, different opportunity, agreed. NYU Shanghai is based on the same overall strategy and structure as NYU Abu Dhabi — a research university into which a liberal arts college is fully integrated. But NYU Shanghai also differs in some respects. The campus is bicultural and multicultural: 50 per cent of its students are Chinese, with the other 50 per cent from outside of China. But the standard for faculty and students is the same as in Abu Dhabi — only the highest level of achievement by all traditional measures, combined with a serious commitment to building a cosmopolitan community at the university and in the world. For example, all the admitted Chinese students not only scored in the very top tier (one per cent) on the test taken by over nine million high school students (the level required by the 'China Nine', China's elite schools) but also passed muster after two days of classes and interviews by the NYU Shanghai admissions team not only verified their intellectual talents but also confirmed their commitment to creating a global community. As in Abu Dhabi, outstanding faculty and students were immediately attracted to this vision. Once again, some of the most respected faculty from NYU New York sought to be involved, and outstanding faculty from other universities left to join the NYU Shanghai team. Of course, the faculty, students, and staff drawn to NYU Shanghai from outside of China are especially interested in China. Those who are from China are attracted to working in an American university, studying alongside brilliant classmates from around the world, and circulating through the global network. As the first class prepared for graduation in 2017, they had been accepted to the very best graduate and professional schools in the world or received job offers at leading companies.

The first decade of NYU's full embrace of its global essence has revealed that to add to the advantages of living in New York City the unique benefits of a university that encourages circulation among the world's idea capitals is an irresistible attraction to many of the smartest people in academe. Even those who do not wish to leave New York City reap the benefits of this model, as scholars from other sites spend time in New York, enhancing academic life at NYU New York. What I have described as the global network university is an advanced form of a university committed at its core to providing an ecumenical model designed to broaden understanding through genuine dialogue. The success of NYU Abu Dhabi and NYU Shanghai, intricately connected with each other and anchored by NYU New York in a worldwide circulatory system, has given proof that such universities are possible and attractive to very talented faculty and students. In the decades ahead, NYU and others who follow this model will modify it and improve upon it, as universities do with every idea.

Bibliography

Kwame Anthony Appiah, *Cosmopolitanism: Ethics in a World of Strangers,* (New York: W.W. Norton & Company, 2006).

A new dawn? Academia moving eastwards

Bertil Andersson

The past 150 years or so has been one of transatlantic academic dominance with a few notable exceptions. Even today, the top of university league tables are still dominated by American and, to a lesser extent, British universities. However, the past decade has seen a fundamental shift in this state of affairs, with an increasing number of Asian universities, both established and new, starting to challenge this 'Western' hegemony. This development reflects the changing nature of global power, especially in terms of economic development, commerce and industry, and military strength. Taken together, this has produced new political trends that impact academia. It certainly belies the popular view of the early 1990s, following the fall of the Berlin Wall, and as enunciated by Francis Fukuyama (1989) as 'The End of History'. Perhaps we are now beyond the 'end'? From an academic perspective, one sees that in 2018, Asia accounted for 26 per cent of the top 50 and 23 per cent of the top 100 universities. For comparison, other than the UK, Europe only accounts for 16 per cent of the top 100 institutions and only six per cent of the top 50 universities (with four from the Netherlands in the top 150 universities). Asia is on the move.

Much of this global change has been due to the rise of China, a giant awakening as a global power not seen since the Tang and Ming dynasties. This is now echoed by modern China as exemplified by its official policy of 'One Belt, One Road' (OBOR) propounded by President Xi Jinping in 2016. China is the second biggest economy in the world as measured by gross domestic product and is on a continuing growth path. It is reflected in academia through such examples as the Xi'an Jiaotong 'Universities Alliance of the Silk Road' that aims to develop a universities alliance along the old Silk Road (see Lie Ma 2016). This also holds for research output, as China is now the second largest producer of academic papers behind the USA and with a rising citation record. Japan remains a significant powerhouse. Even though it has gone through a couple of decades of stagnation, it remains the third largest economy in the world, based on its rapid development especially from the 1960s through to the 1980s. This also applies to its universities, with even the University of Tokyo no longer the leading institution it once was in Asia. Japanese universities suffer from a low international profile and outlook. In contrast, South Korea has seen rapid and aggressive economic growth in recent years, and its universities have shown a parallel increase in global status. It is salutary to remember that in 1960, South Korea had half the gross domestic product of the Republic of South Africa and now has a figure nearly five times as big. Taiwan has experienced a similar growth path with its burgeoning economy leading to increased academic investment. The cities of Hong Kong and Singapore represent new and successful economic models and Singapore, particularly as a city-state without a geographical hinterland, is a highly successful and advanced country standing at the intersection of the East and the West as well as between East Asia and the Asian subcontinent. Both Hong Kong and Singapore have extremely highly ranked universities — probably the highest in the world on a per capita basis. Finally, one has to take into account the emerging Asian economic powers including India, Indonesia, and Vietnam. Together, they have enormous developmental potential, which, eventually, will be reflected in their universities. Their academic sectors remain, as of today, somewhat underdeveloped but with significant potential, especially given the high proportion of young people in their populations, hungry for advanced education.

Looking to the West, the USA remains, for the present, the world's only super-power with its economic and military strength and with its ubiquitous culture permeating most corners of the world. However, even its global leaders such as Apple conduct most of their manufacturing in China and its information technology leaders such as Google and Amazon are now facing strong competition from their Chinese equivalents (Baidu and Tencent, for example). More worryingly, recent events have seen a retreat from some aspects of its global leadership position, not least in its moral and political leadership. Its universities remain strong, particularly its private and 'Ivy League' institutions. Nevertheless, although the USA remains the most powerful country in the world, following recent changes in its political leadership and direction, has a gradual decline already commenced? And how would this affect American academia? For its part, Europe, through the European Union, remains an area of strong and powerful economies. In fact, counting all 28 countries together, this puts the European Union in second place in terms of gross domestic product to the USA, including the fourth, fifth, and sixth largest economies (those of Germany, France, and the UK). However, it continues to be fragmented, with member states always 'flexing their national muscles'. This national mindset continues to bedevil the system in terms of setting priorities. Worryingly, recent years have seen the rise of 'supernationalism' in places such as Hungary and Poland as well as in the Brexit process. Indeed, the potential withdrawal of the United Kingdom from the European Union reflects the same tendencies seen in the USA and is probably the greatest cause for concern. The Union has had to survive a severe financial crisis and now faces fresh challenges in terms of the refugee crisis caused by conflicts on its borders. From an academic viewpoint, Europe's Framework Programme, as an entirety, is the largest research programme in the world. With a British withdrawal from the European Union, this will have a major impact both on the United Kingdom and on mainland European academic institutions. With two of the countries with the most highly ranked universities (Switzerland and the United Kingdom) being outside the European Union, EU-27 universities will not be represented in the top 50 of world universities.

Western (European and North American) universities still predominate in all league tables and bibliometric analyses of institutions of higher education. This follows from European power over the past 150 years (and based on an even longer tradition of learning going back to the first universities of Bologna, Paris, Oxford, and beyond). However, after the Second World War, American institutions came to the fore. Following that war, and with the onset of the Cold War, the centre of gravity of scientific discoveries —measured, for example, by the number of Nobel prize-winners — moved across the Atlantic after a predominance of Germany prior to the Second World War. Coupled with the economic and political challenges posed by Asia, recent political developments in Europe include a return to nationalism, sometimes coloured by racism, and the so-called populist trends. As in the USA, such trends are frequently based on anti-intellectualism (antagonism towards experts). There is also a worrying and increasing disillusionment with democratic systems. Coupled to this is the rise of belief in 'alternative facts' being propagated through social media. Experts, mostly from the universities, are regarded as the cause of problems rather than being seen as part of the solution. There is an increasing lack of confidence in the universities, even though there is now a larger proportion of the entry age cohort attending such institutions compared with the past. Thus, we must recognise that there is an increasing ambivalence in society towards academia. The only discipline that seems to escape this opprobrium is medicine. Asia appears to have escaped much of this populist movement. This is very much a 'Western' phenomenon compared with the high regard in which experts, universities, and learning are held in Asia.

Part of this disillusion has to do with a fear of the future. Historically, this always occurs at a time of dramatic change and uncertainty. The industrial revolution (1.0) based on coal, iron, and steam drove the movement from the country to the cities; the electricity revolution (2.0) that followed was seen by some as a threat to jobs even though it created modern society. This has been followed by the recent information technology revolution (3.0), again accompanied by the same fears. Now we face the challenge of big data, digitisation, robotics, and artificial intelligence (AI) in revolution 4.0, coming so quickly on the heels of the information technology revolution. The likely impact is unclear, but the threats are perceived by society at large. This time the impacts will be felt more widely, with even law, medicine, and accountancy likely to be affected by artificial intelligence, in addition to effects such as driverless vehicles. A feeling of unfairness, partly due to rising inequality, exacerbates such fears. This represents a major challenge for university leaderships. Academic leadership must not hide behind academic dogmas and ivory towers but address these challenges in a flexible manner. It has to convince society at large of the benefits of knowledge to strengthen economies and maintain democratic values. It calls for a better understanding of its learning processes. Maybe we need a second renaissance.

Turning to Asia, we see a growing Asian presence in the top ranks of universities. Scholarly publications increasingly have Asian authors, even though such papers may come from institutions in the USA and Europe. This is accompanied by a rise in the citations from such publications, so that Asians are having an increasing impact on knowledge production. In addition, this represents a change from the old, two-way brain flow across the Atlantic. What we now see is a triangular movement between Asia, Europe, and North America, with Asian universities and institutes not only attracting Asian 'returnees' but also attracting both junior and senior academics from the West. This is particularly evident in the English-speaking cities of Hong Kong and Singapore. This is no accident, as Asian countries devote an increasing share of their gross domestic product to education, research, and development, with Japan and Korea well above the 'magic' three per cent GERD.[1] The USA remains a benchmark at

---

1   GERD stands for Gross Domestic Expenditure on Research and Development as a percentage of the gross domestic product (GDP). It represents the total intramural expenditure on research and development performed in the national territory during a specific reference period (expressed as a percentage of GDP

around 2.5 per cent; Germany is slightly in excess of this with only Finland, Sweden, Switzerland, and Israel substantially exceeding this value. Singapore is around the benchmark level, with ambitions to join these other 'small, smart nations'.

When discussing the rise of Asian universities, Singapore's Nanyang Technological University (NTU) stands out as the most rapidly developing and rising institution. It is ranked eleven in the QS World University Rankings.[2] This has to be seen against the fact that it was only founded as a university in 1991 and primarily was a teaching university (predominantly engineering) until 2000, meeting the needs of Singapore for trained manpower for its manufacturing economy. However, since then it has developed rapidly into a research-intensive university attracting top talent (both senior and junior) from all over the world. NTU benefits from the strong commitment of the Singapore government to the implementation of a knowledge-based economy and its consequent investment in research and the higher education sector. Another advantage enjoyed by NTU is the commitment within Singapore to the whole education system. Education at large is held in high regard in Singapore, and it has an envied school system (topping the OECD PISA league tables in science, mathematics, and reading). NTU and the other Singapore universities thus have a strong 'feeder' system of bright young people. All school teachers are educated at the National Institute of Education (NIE), a world-class institution in teacher education and pedagogical development and an autonomous institute within NTU. The university has revamped its educational programmes to become one of the world's leading technology-enabled educational systems. In its core, engineering, now ranks fourth behind only MIT, Stanford and Cambridge. It has a unique

of the national territory). GERD data taken from the World Economic Outlook Database of October 2017 of the International Monetary Fund, see: https://www.imf.org/external/pubs/ft/weo/2017/02/weodata/index.aspx (accessed 5 February 2018).
2   See: https://www.topuniversities.com/university-rankings/world-university-rankings/2018 (accessed 5 February 2018).

Medical School in an intimate collaboration with Imperial College London, and it conducts top-quality fundamental and applied research. In this latter respect, it has close collaboration and partnership with some of the world's major technology-based multinational companies. Thus, it is hardly surprising that NTU leads the citation impacts in Asia; it is ranked as first amongst young universities (those established within the past fifty years, a list that is now dominated by Asian universities — a clear sign of what we may expect in the future). NTU's unique achievement is not only its rise to become one of the world's strongest universities but the speed of this rise. Other institutions in Asia will surely have the ambition to follow.

In examining global trends, one sees the growth of Asian economies and an increasing assertiveness in their relations with the rest of the world resulting from this new economic power. In turn, this has led to the embrace of the knowledge economy, an increasing commitment to research and knowledge generation and, as a consequence, to higher education and learning. Thus, it is not far-fetched to predict that within the next two decades, Asian universities will have achieved parity with Western universities and that Asia will dominate future, technology-based societies. We should not underestimate such major shifts of power and influence, as they will change the landscape of knowledge and political leadership in the world.

Bibliography

Francis Fukuyama, 'The End of History', *The National Interest*, 16 (1989), pp. 3-18.

Lie Ma, 'University alliance seeks enhanced education co-op along Silk Road', *China Daily*, 11 April 2016.

In search of the South African university — Pages from a Stellenbosch diary

Peter Vale

Day ONE — From a shelf, I take down a book called *Civitas Dei*. This is not *De civitate Dei*, but like Saint Augustine's famous book, this one was written to chart a new understanding of man in the world. The volume in my hand is the second (of three) that broadcast a 'gospel of democracy': published in 1937, it was written by Lionel Curtis, who trained in the Classics and became what today we would call a 'norm-entrepreneur'. The inscription on the title page reads: *'To the Honourable, Dr Malan with every good wish from Abe Bailey, 31 August, 1937'.* Joined together on this page are three white men — Curtis, Malan, Bailey — whose careers helped to chart how it was that South Africa was fashioned as a European state in Africa. To explain: the Utrecht-theology-faculty-trained Malan became the first Afrikaner Nationalist Prime Minister of South Africa (1948); the English-speaking, South African-born Sir Abe Bailey — who had no university training — was a successful businessman, financier, and sometime politician, and inherited the mantle of Cecil John Rhodes, the great champion of the British Empire. These men — and others, of course — used codified knowledge to organize the world around them. And as they did so, they created a form of "the truth". Curtis was spectacularly successful at this: he was instrumental in establishing a chain of institutes across the world; founded an influential academic journal, *The Round Table;* and was core to the founding of International Relations as a distinct field of study in the social sciences. As I close the book, I reflect on how simple — perhaps simple-minded — the making of knowledge was 81 years ago and how intimately — certainly politely, if the inscription is anything to go by — it was spread around: no formal peer review, just the self-confidence of knowing that it was possible to know, and to broadcast, "the truth".

The room is called to order, and my attention turns to the business of the day: I am chairing a workshop to investigate how, if at all, a research programme can be drawn up to address the following challenging topic: 'University and Society: Disruption, Discourse and New Directions'. Our host is STIAS (Stellenbosch Institute for Advanced Study); established thirteen years ago, it has shown how important it is to build (and sustain) free-standing spaces in which "slow scholarship" can promote real understanding — and maybe even "the truth". Finding the creative space that STIAS offers is near impossible in an age of the managerialist university. Two short welcomes are spoken; then, the participants each introduce themselves. This gathering includes several leading local thinkers in the field of higher education but, importantly, there is a mix of young and old — with a good racial and gender balance. We plunge into the business of the first of two days of talking when a bright and increasingly well-known education economist helps the workshop grapple with understanding what statistics we know — or should know — about the post-secondary school sector in South Africa.

A few things quickly become clear: sometimes statistics obfuscate rather than enlighten; there are good statistics on the universities but very few on the technical-training sector of the post-school system; and local universities are not very efficient because it takes much longer than the designated number of years to complete a university degree in South Africa. But, mostly, we agreed that the problem of South African higher education does not lie in generating ever-more statistics.

Day TWO — 6.00 am: A gorgeous morning in the Western Cape. David Hornsby and I walk through the tree-lined suburbs of Stellenbosch towards the Jonkershoek Mountains — we talk politics, family, and, as expected, universities. En route, we pass files of young men dressed in T-shirts who are running in closed ranks;

this is a seasonal thing — it is mid-summer and the academic year has just started. These are university fraternities in their initiation rituals. This particular intake of first-year students will go down in history because it is the centenary year of the founding of Stellenbosch University. A dedicated social scientist, Hornsby recently moved from Johannesburg to the Engineering Faculty of London's University College. Is this trans-disciplinary, trans-continental project what was once known as the globalization of higher education?

The second day of the workshop is devoted to the consideration of several long-term themes, but the two challenges laid down on the first day return again and again. The first challenge is this: 'Who will speak for the universities?' The second challenge is: 'What are universities for?' Some local background is needed to understand the first: in August and September 2016, South Africa's universities were in flames, and the whole structure (many believed at the time) was teetering on the edge of collapse. How? Why? More than twenty-five years after apartheid ended, South African higher education remains embedded within a knowledge world that is remote from the country's majority. It is not that its universities are not universities in the accepted sense of the term, it is just that they seem closer to the world of Lionel Curtis than the South Africa of today. This exclusion led students from the (once wholly white) University of Cape Town, in early 2015, to attack the statue of Cecil John Rhodes, who purportedly was the first benefactor of the university.

The university's leadership responded by removing the statue, but the incident fuelled a movement to 'decolonize knowledge'. Organized around the slogan #RHODESMUSTFALL — the movement spread far and wide, even taking hold at Oxford where Cecil John Rhodes and Lionel Curtis took their respective degrees in the Third Class! These protests were quickly followed by a campaign — which followed students across the world — for free higher education. The mobilizing slogan for this was #FEESMUSTFALL and it spread, like a bushfire, to every university in the country — at times with great destruction to its property. Free access to higher education in South Africa was promised in the iconic 1955 Freedom Charter but has not (until recently) been delivered upon, ostensibly for budgetary reasons. The South African social theorist John Higgins brilliantly summarized the issue in this binary: an Abstract Right promised in another age clashed with Material Conditions of today. We know from history, of course, that this kind of clash has produced the overthrow of many a political regime. As the crisis over fees deepened, however, neither the government nor the broader South African public spoke up in favour of — or showed sympathy for — the universities. It was as if the country's people had lost confidence in the universities and had no patience with the demands of the students!

The second challenge, a global one, is best understood in this doubleheader: 'Every university can easily say what they're good at, but few can tell you what they are good for'. A simple glance at the QS Rankings makes it easy to tell what a university is good at, but what is a university good for? It seems an obvious question, but a quick answer no longer readily trips off the tongue. It wasn't always this way, of course: like Curtis, the first South African universities serviced the needs of British imperialism. The quintessential example was Rhodes University established on a contested frontier called Eastern Cape; it was named after Cecil John Rhodes. Like South Africa's English-medium universities, Rhodes set out to show that the English language and the idea of Empire could successfully bring the country to order. In the late-1920s, South Africa's Afrikaans-medium universities were drawn into the Afrikaner National project — both the language of instruction and academic disciplines were positioned to oppose the imperial project of higher education. This was a case of the labour of higher education operating *for* the nationalist cause — and this, by definition, was against the imperial project. But today in South Africa, these are both spent causes. So, what should South Africa's universities be 'for'?

Like universities everywhere and anywhere, there is no quick answer to this question — no quick answer, certainly but probably no satisfactory answer either. What we know is this: there are deep-seated social and natural science-centred problems facing the country. Climate change suggests itself as one such. This is readily understood here, in Stellenbosch, which is experiencing the driest year since 1933. Restrictions on the use of water are in place, but, as usual, the poor are suffering more than the rich in the face of this crisis. Two decades ago, every one of the three universities here in the Western Cape was developing an institute that was devoted to researching water issues. But, so it seems, none of these was able to predict —let alone help plan for — the water crisis, which is now on everyone's tongue. Can these still help, or should the universities be exploring what, if any, solutions may be on offer by an indigenous knowledge system?

The day ends with a list of things to do written on the white board — and the inevitable agreement that, to understand the university, let alone change it, we will have to meet again. Is this what the university is 'for' — endless meetings? Or will this workshop be different?

The labyrinth of EU research, innovation, and education policy

Kurt Deketelaere

Vice-chancellor of Utrecht University Bert van der Zwaan, also chairman of the League of European Research Universities (LERU), is retiring in a crucial year for Europe's research, innovation, and education policy. The next elections for the European Parliament are due to be held just over a year from the moment of writing this essay: in May 2019. Later that same year, a new European Commission will take over with a new president, as Jean-Claude Juncker has said he will stand down. The European Union will also need to find a new President of the European Council, as Donald Tusk will reach the end of his term in November 2019; unless, as Juncker proposed recently, one person is going to take up both jobs. The upshot is that 2019 will be fully booked with campaigning, elections, appointments and transition periods. Any policy development and decision-making will therefore have to happen in the next ten to twelve months. This means that European Union institutions are facing some crucial decisions in 2018. To mention just three: the future of the Union; the future of EU finances; and the United Kingdom's membership of the European Union. Major progress must be made on all three in the coming weeks. Further delay on any would endanger timely decision-making in several policy fields, including research, innovation, and education.

For example, the successors to the Horizon 2020 and Erasmus+ programmes must be developed, consulted on, and finalized before the parliamentary elections. Informal consultations on these programmes have been going on for a while, but the timeframe is becoming more worrying by the day. A formal proposal for the next multi-annual financial framework — set to run from 2021 to, presumably, 2027 — is now expected by May 2018. This is essential if there is to be a formal proposal for the next Framework programme in June 2018. Given the political calendar, it seems optimistic to hope that Framework 9 will be announced, negotiated, and signed off before the parliamentary elections. That raises the worrying possibility that the next cohort of members of the European Parliament and Commissioners will seek to impose differing views of research, innovation and education. The wrap-up of Phase 1 of the Brexit negotiations, which covers citizens' rights, financial commitments, and the Irish border, raised the hope that EU budget discussions would speed up significantly. How much will the United Kingdom pay the European Union for its present commitments? Will it contribute financially to specific policy fields post-Brexit such as research, education, and innovation, and if so, how much? Hoping for fast and clear answers to these questions was seemingly unjustified due to the difficult negotiations on the transition period and the legal write-up of the Phase 1 agreement. Nonetheless, transparency on financial matters is key for all member states and for all present and future policy issues. For Framework 9, the crucial requirement is clear: a significant budget increase as requested by the Lamy Report, the Tallinn Call for Action, the League of European Research Universities and many others. It was good to see that the Budget Commissioner recently already indicated that, for him, the next Multi-annual Financial Framework (MFF) would not cut into research and education budgets but, on the contrary, increase them. Not only for budgetary reasons but also for reasons of content, collaboration, and the programme's success, it is essential that the United Kingdom remains on board. If that means revising the rules on association with the Framework programme, so be it (see below).

As well as implementing Horizon 2020 and shaping Framework 9, further implementation of the policies on open science and open innovation will remain important in 2018. In May, the Competitiveness Council will receive a detailed briefing on the eight open-science priorities. Hopefully this will include significant progress on setting up the European Open Science Cloud and the Open Access Publications Platform. On open innovation, it is crucial that the regulatory environment in the EU improves. Better-focused and organized EU policies and a more harmonized EU legal framework on taxation, intellectual property, and bankruptcy are essential; a European Innovation Council or Agency is not. The EU must also give the creation of the European Research Area (ERA) a further boost in 2018. The idea that the treaty obligations on the ERA have been fulfilled is an illusion; the free circulation of knowledge and researchers is a long way from being reality. In fact, more and more obstacles have been introduced through various legislative frameworks such as data protection and copyright. And although the ERA is a work in progress, the European Union has just launched another area, the European Education Area (EEA). At present, there is a nice set of proposals and ideas (European Universities Networks, European Student Card, Mutual Recognition of Degrees, et cetera), but without legislative back up and sufficient funding, they will remain soft and difficult to realize. It looks as if the wishful thinking of French President Emmanuel Macron has been contagious.

Almost eighteen months after the Brexit referendum, we all agree with British actor Hugh Grant's observation: 'Brexit was a fantastic example of a nation shooting itself full in the face'. Slogans of the pro-Brexit camp such as 'Brexit means Brexit' or 'Taking back control' has proven to be a complete failure. A lack of vision, knowledge, preparation, and political leadership have brought the United Kingdom to the edge of the worst-case scenario: a 'no deal' Brexit. The unanimous position and consequent negotiation strategy of the EU 27 have led to a full 'capitulation' of the United Kingdom in Phase 1 of the Brexit negotiations: offering a significant financial commitment, a final say of the European Court of Justice on citizens' rights, and guarantees for a soft Irish border, convinced the EU 27 in December 2017 of 'sufficient progress made' and the possibility to move to the second phase of Brexit negotiations, focusing on the future co-operation between the UK and EU. For research, innovation, and education, the start of this second phase is absolutely necessary and crucial. Phase 1 only had 'limited' relevance: guarantees for the continued participation of the United Kingdom in Horizon 2020 and Erasmus+ until the end of the present multi-annual financial framework; and guaranteeing the rights as citizens of British researchers in continental Europe and, vice versa, of European (continental) nationals in the United Kingdom. And although 'limited', this has proven to be already very difficult. Reports indicate that the participation and success of the UK in Horizon 2020 is declining, and worrying amounts of students and researchers have left the country or do not come or apply to institutions in the UK anymore. Clearly, it is time for action.

In Phase 2, the United Kingdom will indeed have to put its research cards on the table. In its September 2017 *Future Partnership* paper called *Collaboration on Science and Innovation*, the British government stated: 'Given the UK's unique relationship with European science and innovation, the UK would also like to explore forging a more ambitious and close partnership with the EU than any yet agreed between the EU and a non-EU country'. This is a nice and reassuring message, in the first place for British and other UK-based researchers. The question is, of course, whether it is a realistic position. Next to the fact that the Future Partnership paper is a perfect public relations document for the outstanding research being conducted in the United Kingdom, it also suffers from wishful thinking, window dressing, and impossible interpretations of EU law when it comes down to a possible future partnership with the EU. What is a better partnership than, for example, the one the European Union already has with non-EU countries like Israel, Switzerland, or Norway? Indeed, EU membership is the better option, but the whole issue is that this is what the UK wants to get rid of. Is it an option then to become an EFTA country? This option has already been ruled out twice — very explicitly — by UK Prime Minister Theresa May herself. Or perhaps become a so-called Neighbourhood country? The United Kingdom evidently does not even want to consider this option. However, the three above-mentioned options (EU member state, EFTA country, Neighbourhood country) are the only ones according to Horizon 2020 that give access to the status of a country 'associated' with the framework programme. And although even this notion of 'associated membership' seems unacceptable to the United Kingdom, it is a key condition for ERC grantees, who need to stay in an EU member state or associated country for up to six months or a year in order to be in compliance with their grant conditions. So becoming a third country and not being associated with Horizon 2020 or Framework Programme 9 is a nightmare for UK-based ERC grantees or new grantees planning to go with their grant to the United Kingdom. It bears the threat of a significant brain drain from the UK to the EU 27 and the Horizon 2020-associated countries. And of course, we do not want brain drain but brain circulation, cross-border collaboration, multi-national teams, all including the United Kingdom, in order to bring the best researchers together to solve societal problems.

A possible solution to this dilemma was launched earlier by the League of European Research Universities (LERU) and was picked up more explicitly by the LAMY group where its report states the following as recommendation 10: 'Make international R&I cooperation a trademark of EU research and innovation; Action: open up the R&I programme to *association by the best and participation by all*, based on reciprocal co-funding or access to co-funding in the partner country.' Although the official narrative is that this is a way to bring strong research countries like Canada and Australia on board of the framework programme, it is clear this also opens the door for a global research power like the United Kingdom. So, instead of getting the UK in one of the three above-mentioned groups of countries for association, let us change the rules for association to and participation in the programme. Obviously this will require the United Kingdom to input money into the EU budget, to use European Commission contracts, and to accept the authority of the European Court of Justice and the decision-making power of the EU 27 when it concerns research policy. Suggesting a kind of 'association+' whereby the associated strong non-EU research countries also have a formal say in the EU policy development and decision-making process will perhaps be a bridge too far for the EU 27, although it certainly could have added value in the case of the UK.

UK universities and research institutes are fully aware of all these issues. It is unclear to what extent the British government really is, notwithstanding the above-mentioned Future Partnership paper. Is the British government conscious of the destructive consequences of its 'policy' of the past twenty-plus months, not only for universities but for British society as a whole? Surely, vice-chancellors from British higher education institutions, with the explicit support of their continental colleagues, must and will increase the pressure in the following days, weeks, and months, in order to reach an 'acceptable' Brexit deal by the summer of 2018. After all, they are among the few societal forces left that can speak up and guide this country in these extremely challenging times. But — who can tell — perhaps none of the above will be necessary. Perhaps common sense will return in the United Kingdom and through new elections or a new referendum or a parliamentary vote, Brexit will not take place in the end. Just keep in mind how even the Swiss changed their minds after two years. Day by day, it becomes clear to all British citizens that Brexit does not mean Brexit and that taking back control actually means losing control. Let us see when the flipping point is reached.

Unlike the government of the United Kingdom, Bert van der Zwaan has prepared Utrecht University and the League of European Research Universities (LERU) in a perfect way for the challenging times ahead. For LERU, he has been a fantastic chair and a great supporter and promoter of the League. His no-nonsense approach, impressive knowledge and strategic vision of the professional field, clear target setting, and great people management have clearly reinforced LERU's position and reputation at both the EU and the member state level.

Part 5

Reflections on institutional logic

Academic enterprise as a new institutional logic for *public* higher education

Michael Crow, Derrick Anderson, and Kyle Whitman

Few themes in the study of human affairs are as enduring as the origins and functions of *public* institutions. Classic perspectives including those pertaining to collective action, the division of labour, and Weber's bureaucratic model of organization (Weber 1934) have been complimented by more modern economic and behavioural theories of the firm (Cyert & March 2006) and assorted theories of the political economy of organizations (Wamsley & Zald 1973). All of these perspectives, and many more, are united by a common recognition that society requires *public* institutions. And yet today, in practice, there are few examples of industries that are purely public (Wilson 1989). Accordingly, to account for the dynamic influences of economic, social, and political forces that shape so-called 'public' institutions, today's scholars and institutional designers rely on contingent frameworks including those related to publicness (Bozeman 1987; Talmage et al. 2018, forthcoming), public-private hybrid organizations (Emmert & Crow 1988; Koppell 2010), and public-private partnerships (Girth et al. 2012; Warner & Hefetz 2008). With this background, the logic of 'academic enterprise' proposed here recognizes the practical and theoretical significance of the dynamic and changing nature of public higher education.

Universities are important within the context of public organizations. In a simple legal sense, many universities are public as a consequence of their constitutional or legislative charters (Rudulf 1962). The social functions of universities as instruments of knowledge production and dissemination amount to a clear public purpose. Yet, these organizations experience widely different levels of government control relative to other public organizations: some universities are able to set their own goals and priorities while others are able only to determine methods for achieving organizational goals set by other governance structures (Hutchens 2008). Thus, universities are legally, structurally, and functionally public but may offer a design space to experiment with organizational models and logics. As scholars and designers of public organizations working in higher education, we are keenly interested in the history, evolution, and future of public universities, however they are conceptualized.

There are currently a variety of organizational models and institutional logics in higher education. But if the public nature and function of a university is inherent, the reliance on any particular model is a design choice. As with any design choice, there are limits to its relevance and effectiveness. The predominant academic bureaucratic model — characterized by rigidity, formalization and specialization — has proven to be useful in many instances, but it is increasingly seen as a barrier to the enhanced social and economic impact many universities aspire to realize. As Anthony Downs (1967) argues, public bureaus in general are inclined to an organizational logic of self-preservation rooted in dependency upon the state: 'Once the users of the bureau's services have become convinced of their gains from it, and have developed routinized relations with it, the bureau can rely upon a certain amount of inertia to keep on generating the external support it needs.' Universities, even as they are often legally or functionally public, need not operate according to a bureaucratic institutional logic. One alternative operational paradigm is that of the *academic enterprise.* In my experience, turning to the academic enterprise model can empower universities to achieve new levels of excellence in teaching and discovery while providing greater economic and social value. Scholars have identified several institutional logics in higher education that structure behaviours and expectations of actors both in and outside of higher education organizations (Leslie & Johnson 1974; Clark 1983). The table builds on and extends the currently conceptualized academic logics, academic bureaucracy logics, and market logics and introduces the academic enterprise model. Although these are idealized types that are rarely, if ever, observed in practice, they are still relevant to the extent to which they guide administrative behaviour, constructions of organizational performance, and policy agendas.

MINANT AND EMERGING INSTITUTIONAL LOGICS IN HIGHER EDUCATION

	Academic	Academic Bureaucracy	Market	Academic Enterprise
Animating Purpose	Enlightenment of individual students	Organizational preservation	Profit maximization for owners and shareholders	Social transformation
Path to Achieving Public Value	Immersive instruction	Achievement of state-specified goals	Efficiency and cost reduction	Connecting instruction to knowledge generation at society-impacting scale
sumptions of Faculty	Self-governing professionals	Bureaucrats responding to rules	Commodity labor; faculty not entrepreneurial	Knowledge entrepreneurs
sumptions of Management	Management drawn from and blended with faculty	Traditional public managers distinct from faculty	Professional management distinct from faculty and acting entrepreneurially	Management drawn from and blended with faculty but acting entrepreneurially
ccountability Mechanisms	Faculty and Management Professionalism	Audits, public reporting, standardized testing	Student choice, standardized testing	Demonstrated economic and social progress
mary Funding Mechanisms	Enrollment funding from state, endowments	Enrollment funding from state	Vouchers, performance based funding from state	Diverse; institutional entrepreneurship
rganizational ale of Impact	Individual or groups of individuals	Community or state	Indeterminate, any scale from which profit can be derived	Social scale with possible national and global reach

The academic model views the autonomous, self-governing organization as the organizational ideal and prioritizes the traditional, higher-education values of elitism and excellence. For generations, universities operating in this model have benefited from generous state support and large endowments that subsidize niche learning experiences. Accountability is ensured by the professionalism of the faculty. These universities are characterized by low acceptance rates, high tuition rates, and a small scale.

Most public universities operate in the academic bureaucratic model. Although this organizational logic is familiar to government principals overseeing executive and legislative agencies, there are significant drawbacks when this logic is deployed in the context of higher education. First, academic bureaucracies *operate according to a narrow and sometimes misplaced interpretation of efficiency.* Efficiency for a bureaucracy is a managerial undertaking within the context of a self-imposed institutional conserver mandate. Second, academic bureaucracies are often *overly concerned with the external political environment,* striving not only to comply or over-comply with the law but also to ensure that their actions do nothing to change their relationships with external stakeholders. Often, the focus on maintaining stakeholder relations comes at the expense of improving or reinventing these relations. Third, academic bureaucracies are generally *risk averse,* seeking to conserve a scarce allotment of resources, even at the expense of quality in teaching, learning, and research. More specifically, a consequence of being accountable to assorted external stakeholders including legislators, regulators, and donors, academic bureaucracies tend to adopt conserver mentalities when using resources instead of investor mentalities. All the shortcomings described here are interrelated.

By defining their publicness as a function of their legal status or source of resources rather than by a higher mission to achieve beneficial social outcomes in spite of political constraints, the operations of public universities sometimes adopt some of the more vexing attributes of public bureaucracies. Many have become hierarchical, rigid, rule-bound, and change-resistant.

More concerning, many public universities have lost their way by becoming responsive primarily to the narrow mandates prescribed by external stakeholders and by privileging a narrowly defined conceptualization of managerial efficiency rather than the maximization of social impact. The consequences include a limited capacity to respond to emerging social and technological changes, which, in turn, result in lower-quality learning and discovery outcomes. While a small number of public universities are able to maintain or enhance excellence in teaching and research, they often do so at the expense of accessibility while succumbing to the magnetism of rankings and relative institutional status.

In recent years, governments have designed policies that inject market mechanisms into higher education in the hope of ultimately changing organizational logics and increasing performance. These policies, such as the Pell grant programme, often focus on transforming students into consumers by subsidizing their purchase decisions and turning universities into providers that attract student consumers. These policies have had broad implications at existing universities such as altered faculty-administration relationships, but have also coincided with the emergence of for-profit organizations that seek to use public funds to capitalize on new student markets. Theoretically, these market-driven organizations are held accountable by the forces of student choice. Unfortunately, organizations operating in this logic expend considerable sums on advertising and often offer lower quality, commodified education (Anderson & Taggart 2016). However, underperforming for-profit organizations are seldom pushed out of the market, undermining the argument that a market functioning on subsidized student choice can provide meaningful discipline or accountability. Academic bureaucracies, in contrast, often combine access with efficiency at the expense of innovation and excellence. They largely opt against defining their own outcomes and respond first and foremost to accountability mechanisms dictated by the state. In this context, the challenge for ambitious public universities is to define and achieve differentiated outcomes, regardless of the political and financial constraints with which they must contend.

As an alternative to academy logics, academic bureaucracy logics, and market logics, our own institution, Arizona State University (ASU), has adopted the *academic enterprise* model to pursue excellence in outcomes and enhanced effectiveness in access. Under the academic enterprise model, public universities like ASU continue to receive state support and maintain public purpose, but also take responsibility for innovating, adapting, and differentiating themselves from other institutions according to the unique needs of their community and social context. Academic enterprises therefore can be identified as public because they achieve economic and social progress in the public interest. As enterprises, they cultivate multiple sources of revenue through collaborative partnerships, commercialization of research, spin-offs, and novel reconfigurations of business operations. Public academic enterprises lessen their dependency upon the state by treating the state as one of many key investors. Bound neither by inertia nor by fear of external pressures and resource constraints, the academic enterprise defines success on its own terms and charts its trajectory accordingly. The responsibility of the academic enterprise is to ensure a sufficient return on investment for the state. The transition to a model of academic enterprise requires a strong entrepreneurial vision at the executive level that is dis-seminated and adopted throughout the university. Rather than becoming more centralized, leadership becomes more diffuse, as faculty and administrators take ownership for achieving better outcomes by acting as *knowledge entrepreneurs* rather than as bureaucratic functionaries. Although public academic enterprises continue to value efficiency, the rationale for efficient operations shifts from a model of 'doing the best we can with scarce resources' towards maximizing effectiveness and elevating the quality of the university's core activities of teaching and discovery. Rather than seeking to achieve the minimum acceptable outcomes as defined by the state, and at the lowest possible cost, public academic enterprises encourage risk-taking that works towards the university's unique mission. The academic enterprise model affords public universities with the resources to offer value to its stakeholders at scale rather than treating knowledge as a luxury good that is limited to the few. It gives public universities the ability to provide access without sinking into mediocrity and to achieve excellence without restricting admissions.

Is a transition to the academic enterprise model attainable for most public universities? Arizona State University's transformation over the last sixteen years, which took place despite major systemic and budgetary obstacles, should inspire confidence. Through strategic organizational streamlining designed to cut costs while preserving the quality of the academic core, ASU has become one of the nation's most efficient producers of both college graduates and high impact, socially meaningful research. ASU's cost per degree is nearly 20 per cent below the national median. Enrolment has risen from 55,491 undergraduate, graduate, and professional students in the fall semester of 2002 to 103,039 in 2017 — roughly an 85 per cent increase. This includes more than 30,000 degree-seeking online learners. The number of degrees awarded has increased from 11,803 during the academic year of 2002–2003 to 23,334 in 2016-2017. Total minority enrolment from the fall of 2002 through the fall of 2016 soared by 202 per cent from 11,487 to 34,699. Minority enrolment now comprises more than 35 per cent of the total. These achievements demonstrate ASU's capacity to deliver its legacy mission of access at great efficiency. But in doing so, ASU has also established new capacities that enhance its ability in terms of excellence. ASU is among the top ten public universities in its enrolment of National Merit Scholars, enrolling more than Stanford, MIT, Duke, Brown, or the University of California, Berkeley. ASU is also among the top three producers of Fulbright Scholars in the nation, tied with Princeton and Rutgers and coming in behind only Harvard and the University of Michigan.

As a consequence of an ambitious expansion of the research enterprise, research-related expenditures over the period FY 2002 to FY 2016 have grown by more than a factor of four — without significant growth in the size of the faculty — reaching a record of $518 million in FY 2016, up from $123 million in FY 2002. The estimated figure for FY 2017 is more than $540 million. According to the most recent data from the National Science Foundation (2016 HERD survey), ASU ranks ninth of 718 universities without medical schools in terms of total research expenditures — ahead of Caltech, Princeton, and Carnegie Mellon. The ASU faculty now includes four Nobel laureates and more members of the National Academies than have served on the faculty during the entire history of the institution, including eight members of the National Academy of Engineering, eleven members of the National Academy of Sciences, and two members of the Institute of Medicine.

ASU's public mission means that comparisons between ASU and other major research universities must be appreciated within the context of our commitment to accessibility. ASU admits all Arizona students who have the ability of doing university level work. This means enrolment of freshman classes numbering more than 12,000 that correlate with the socioeconomic and ethnic diversity of our region. These achievements demonstrate that a state-supported university can realize ambitious transformation even as the state withdraws its support. In our case, the state of Arizona has reduced general fund appropriations for its three state universities from $1.07 billion in 2008 to $681 million in 2017, but ASU has managed to grow and thrive through entrepreneurial pursuits that create a diverse base of operational funding. Arizona State University is proof that the academic enterprise model can succeed, which offers a path for public universities to escape dependency upon the state and achieve excellence without restricting access. Not all public universities need to follow ASU's specific pathway to success — on the contrary, the academic enterprise model will look different for every institution. By allowing institutions to grow and thrive on their own terms, freed from artificial constraints that bind public bureaus, academic enterprise offers public higher education institutions not only a way out of state dependency but also a path towards differentiated development according to the needs of the communities that they are mandated to serve.

Bibliography

Derrick M. Anderson and Gabel Taggart, 'Organizations, Policies, and the Roots of Public Value Failure: The Case of For-Profit Higher Education', *Public Administration Review*, 76(5) (2016), pp. 779-789.

Barry Bozeman, *All organizations are public: Bridging public and private organizational theories* (San Francisco: Jossey-Bass Publishers, 1987).

Burton R. Clark, *The Higher Education System: Academic Organization in Cross-national Perspective* (Berkeley: University of California Press, 1983).

Richard M. Cyert and James G. March, 'A behavioral theory of the firm', in John B. Miner (ed.), *Organizational Behavior 2: Essential Theories of Process and Structure* (New York: M.E. Sharp, 2006), pp. 60-77.

Anthony Downs, *Inside Bureaucracy* (New York: RAND Corporation, 1967).

Mark A, Emmert and Michael M. Crow, 'Public, Private and Hybrid Organizations An Empirical Examination of the Role of Publicness', *Administration & Society* 20 (2) (1988), pp. 216-244.

Amanda M. Girth, Amir Hefetz, Jocelyn M. Johnston, and Mildred E. Warner, 'Outsourcing public service delivery: Management responses in non-competitive markets', *Public Administration Review* 72 (6) (2012), pp. 887-900.

Neal H. Hutchens, 'Preserving the Independence of Public Higher Education: An Examination of State Constitutional Autonomy Provisions for Public Colleges and Universities', *Journal of College and University Law* 35 (2008), pp. 271-322.

Jonathan Koppell, 'Administration without borders', *Public Administration Review* 70 (1) (2010), pp. 46-55.

Larry L. Leslie and Gary P. Johnson, 'The market model and higher education', *The Journal of Higher Education* 45(1) (1974), pp. 1-20.

Frederick Rudolph, *The American College and University: A History* (Atlanta: University of Georgia Press, 1962).

Gary L. Wamsley and Mayer N. Zald, 'The political economy of public organizations', *Public Administration Review* 33 (1) (1973), pp. 62-73.

Mildred E. Warner and Amir Hefetz, 'Managing markets for public service: The role of mixed public–private delivery of city services', *Public administration review* 68 (1) (2008), pp. 155-166.

Max Weber, *Die Protestantische Ethik und der Geist des Kapitalismus* (Tübingen: Mohr, 1934).

Talmage, C.; Anderson, D.; and Searle, Mark. Whither recreation and parks? Understanding the decline of public institutions through a preliminary theory of adaptive publicness. *Perspectives on Public Management and Governance.* (2018, forthcoming).

Wilson, J.Q. (1989). *Bureaucracy: What government agencies do and why they do it.* Basic Books.

Don't be scared; be prepared

Barbara Baarsma

More and more people are in paid employment. And that is very good news. Because having a job is about more than having an income. It is an important factor for happiness and for well-being. Richard Layard, co-founder of the annual World Happiness Report, calculated in 2011 that having paid work is in third place in the top seven factors that form the basis for happiness. This is not such a crazy idea because a job — whether you are working for a boss or self-employed — gives meaning to your life. Not having a job seems to have an even greater effect on our happiness than could be inferred from the third place on Layard's list. It turns out that people can get used to being divorced or their health deteriorating but not to unemployment. Any person who has ever been unemployed for longer than six months is permanently unhappier. Seen in this light, you would wish that everyone could have a paid job. Yet this is prevented by our outdated labour market policy. In the meantime, the labour market is changing rapidly under the influence of technological developments and globalization. The use of new technology in particular is leading to deindustrialization and a shift towards a service economy. Not only are people more often faced with compulsory job changes as a result of technological developments but also the rising of the retirement age coupled with longer life expectancy means we are all staying in employment for far longer. So it is a cause for concern that workers do not realize the vital importance of lifelong learning.

Without investing in human capital throughout the working life, there is no job security in the labour market of the twenty-first century. No-one can get by any longer with an educational or training programme at the start of their working life and then nothing more until their retirement. A person finishing vocational training with a diploma at the age of 21 and then entering the labour market will have to work for more than fifty years before they can collect their state pension. This is just not possible with a single study or training programme. We will all have to return to the classroom from time to time for additional training or reskilling. Because the developments in the labour market particularly affect those who have taken secondary vocational education, I had dozens of talks with these kinds of students last year. In my conversations with these students, I suggested that they ask their grandparents what kinds of jobs were available to them fifty years ago. Do these jobs still exist today? Many of those former professions have long disappeared: telegram deliverer, servant, knife grinder, coal man, switchboard operator, and data typist. It is just as insightful to look at the connection between the education the grandparents received back then and the jobs that are available now, such as data scientist, cyber security expert, drone traffic controller, data hostage specialist, or remote healthcare specialist. This connection is not there. I then asked the students if they thought their current education would mean they are ready for the jobs that will be around in fifty years' time. No, of course not. They would be no more ready than you or I would be. So how can we prepare the labour market for the twenty-first century? Modern labour market policy is focused on work security. An activating approach encourages people to maintain their skills in order to be assured of work throughout their career. It also stimulates employers to make time and resources available for this.

One aspect of modern labour market policy is the introduction of a single form of contract. Everyone is given a standard contract for five years, for example (Baarsma 2017). This gives workers who now move from one temporary job to another more security, although this doesn't mean there will be no more contracts that are shorter than five years in duration. In order to meet the flexible need for a temporary workforce, temporary agency staff will still be used, for example. And even after the introduction of a five-year contract, it will still be possible to fire people who do not function adequately. After the introduction of the five-year contract, there will be no more permanent contracts. Of course, this means that those people who now have a permanent contract will lose some security, but they will gain something else in its place. Employees who now have a permanent contract may lose (supposed) job security, but they will invest in work security. At present, people are really only confronted by knowledge obsolescence if they lose their job or are under threat of this. And that is often too late. However, the five-year contract will stimulate all workers to continue to grow and develop. By the time the contract is nearing its end, the worker will be forced to take stock: do I still like this job? Am I as productive as I was a couple of years ago? What skills do I lack? It also keeps the employer sharp. When the contract ends, he asks himself: am I still sufficiently attractive as an employer? Do I provide enough challenge for the employee? Does my company offer enough opportunities to progress? In this way, workers are continually stimulated to invest in their work productivity and they remain attractive for the labour market, and employers are stimulated to support lifelong learning.

Don't get me wrong: I do not see the five-year contract as an end in itself but as a means to stimulate people to continue to invest in their knowledge and skills. In every debate I have participated, I have yet to encounter a better means of making people truly resilient in the labour market of the twenty-first century. The five-year contract is not a stand-alone solution but is linked to the idea of compulsory insurance for all workers against knowledge obsolescence. Rapid technological developments mean that unemployment may become more persistent. People who are unable to adapt or lack the capacity for additional training or reskilling will be the victims of progress. This demands a new kind of social security because not everyone has the resources for additional training or reskilling, and employers will not be willing to invest in education for everyone. This applies to groups of elderly workers, the long-term unemployed, and people with an occupational impairment. For this reason, I advocate setting up an insurance against knowledge obsolescence. This insurance would take the place of the present fragmented educational facilities, which are largely inaccessible to the self-employed and to temporary workers. The insurance would be mandatory for all workers and could only be called upon in the event of a labour market transition that requires substantial additional training or reskilling. The starting capital could be drawn from the money sitting in the over 1,000 subsidy funds that remains unused.

Simultaneously with the implementation of a modern labour market policy, the government needs to ensure sufficient competition regulation of the education market. Almost 85 per cent of people aged between 15 and 64 taking post-initial education do this at a private, non-government-funded institution (Rosenboom & Tieben 2015). Besides private institutions, public institutions also offer education to workers and jobseekers. These are research universities, universities of applied sciences, and regional vocational training centres. They are funded by the government to provide initial education. This creates a non-level playing field, because public funds that are intended for initial education are also used to provide post-initial education (Baarsma 2010). As far back as 2003, the Ministry of Education, Culture and Science in the Netherlands laid down rules to properly regulate the private activities of publicly funded institutions. In the memorandums *Helderheid in de bekostiging van het hoger onderwijs* (Clarity in the funding of higher education) and *Helderheid in de bekostiging van het beroepsonderwijs en de volwasseneneducatie* (Clarity in the funding of vocational/higher professional education and adult education), the ministry attempted to formulate criteria that the funded institutions could use to determine when cross-subsidization from the initial education to the post-initial education market is permitted. However, these memorandums did not bring the clarity promised in their titles. The assessment criteria were too broad for this, and the monitoring of compliance insufficiently specifically aimed at preventing the distortion of competition. The lack of clarity in the rules means that the institutions do not feel constrained by them. The scope allowed by the Clarity memorandums is increasingly used by publicly funded educational institutions (Baarsma 2015). Sometimes the cross-subsidization is implicit. For example, teachers who work in initial education may provide post-initial education at a reduced rate or not charge for their preparation time. And the costs of materials, accommodation, and other overheads for the post-initial teaching may be masked by counting them mainly in the subsidized initial part instead of calculating them wholly or in part in the rates for the post-initial education.

What difference does it make if publicly funded institutions can distort competition? Of course, it is not about competition in itself but the effect of competition. For participants in education, competition generates the best quality, service, and price and a wide variety. Modern labour policy sharpens the incentive for lifelong learning, and effective competition policy ensures a varied range of good quality and reasonably priced educational programmes.

Bibliography

Barbara E. Baarsma, 'Beyond the myth of job security and permanent contract: On the road to work security' (in Dutch), *Special RaboResearch*, 14 November 2017.

Barbara E. Baarsma, 'Five-year contract as part of a five-point plan for the labour market' (in Dutch), *Het Financieele Dagblad*, 11 May 2017, p. 9.

Barbara E. Baarsma, 'Education, market, and state' (in Dutch), *Economisch Statistische Berichten,* 100(4717), p. 523.

Barbara E. Baarsma, 'Competition problems in the education market at the cost of the knowledge economy' (in Dutch), *Economisch Statistische Berichten*, 95(4596), p. 669.

Nicole Rosenboom and Bert Tieben, *Market monitor of private education providers of vocational programmes and training* (in Dutch), (Amsterdam: SEO Amsterdam Economics, 2015).

The idea of the university:
National asset or ivory tower?[1]

Huang Hoon Chng

I am privileged to be part of this project to honour Professor Bert van der Zwaan as he steps down as the vice-chancellor of Utrecht University this year. I met Professor Van der Zwaan in 2017 and was introduced to his book, *Higher Education in 2040 — A Global Approach* (2017). Since then, I have revisited this wonderful book many times. This essay is inspired by Bert van der Zwaan's ideas, picking up on just one thread: the very important but difficult question of 'the idea of the university' in the face of both present and future challenges. He indicates that this matter will require broad debate: '... a debate in which society and the university look one another squarely in the eye to discuss the question of what would be desirable in future, not only for the university, but also for society'. (Van der Zwaan 2017: 8)[2] Are universities ivory towers or national assets? In my view, this is a *false* dichotomy — one does not preclude the other. A caveat: the phrase, '*the* university' suggests a homogeneous entity, but as Van der Zwaan has correctly pointed out, 'The university does not exist and there are many differences in the national contexts' (p. 29). Hence '*the* university' is at best an abstraction, and 'the idea' of the university is only an idea, or an imagined state of affairs. For the rest of this essay, while we will allude to '*the* university', it is crucial to bear in mind that universities across the world may prioritize different roles and purposes.

---

1   A 2011 University of Cambridge Public Lecture Series addressed the issue, "What are universities for?" and the universities minister David Willetts was quoted characterizing universities as "one of our great national assets" (see Swain 2011).
2   Unless otherwise stated, all page references in my essay refer to the Van der Zwaan book.

The idea of the university, and what it is for, is not a new debate (cf. Newman 1907; Boulton & Colin 2008; Pelikan 1992; Collini 2012). The role of the university is a critical question indeed, and we should keep it in view because what our institution is for goes to the heart of our academic identities. Perhaps we only ask, 'What are universities for?' when we feel ourselves under siege, with the dramatic changes in both the internal (e.g. changes in funding models; government pressures and calls from public stakeholders for more accountability) and external (e.g. new technological challenges; growing competition for talent across institutions) environments. At most other times, life goes on in universities — we teach, conduct research, and we worry constantly about balancing teaching, research, service, *and* family life. We do not often stop to ask, 'How should we respond as students, as faculty members, or as academic leaders to the changes swirling around us?'

Globalization has made its effects felt in education. While many academics have benefited from global access to networks and information, the increased competition for talent and on league tables have translated into performance pressures. Many academics are also lamenting that universities are increasingly shaped by economics and funding models and that the university feels like a 'massive grey [teaching] factory' (p. 177). With rapid technological developments, the 'digital' university and the unbundling of curriculum have become all too real. Adding to this is the problem of widening social inequalities and the need for social restructuring in many economies. In Singapore, for example, calls from the very top of government to an entire population to engage in lifelong learning has gained momentum, with SkillsFuture — a lifelong learning funding framework — providing the additional training for individuals who need to rethink a career pathway or reskill. All Singapore universities have been asked to contribute their expertise to this initiative. Singapore's *The Sunday Times* recently devoted a full-page report (Tang 2018: 3 articles) discussing alternatives (i.e. models, pathways, pedagogy) to 'traditional teaching method[s]' in tertiary institutions, in response to this new education/social landscape. One piece entitled 'Uni model should develop critical, creative thinking' is just one among many that powers today's discussion in higher education circles about how universities can respond to an uncertain future by focusing on life skills and competencies. While some of us may feel that the university has become too much of an enterprise, in the case of Singapore, it is an aging population together with the projected misalignment of skills to future jobs and not money that are the primary drivers. While the idea of the university as entrepreneurial may be unpalatable to many academics, with these changes in the external environment, the university has a responsibility to be more socially engaged, 'to enable higher education to demonstrate value beyond the "ivory tower"' (Smidt & Sursock cited in Van der Zwaan, p. 154) or risk losing its connection to society.

Here, I pause to highlight a few important points. First of all, the university does not exist in a vacuum, as an *a priori* entity. The university is a social institution, among many, within society. I do not think we can ignore societal calls for universities to contribute in ways that are more relevant to our society. In Singapore, for example, perhaps due to the small size of the city-state, the universities work closely with industry and government bodies and directly contribute to the Singapore economy. As Van der Zwaan puts it, '[t]here is no splendid isolation' (p. 125) in the Singaporean context. The link to industry and the state means that Singapore universities are state-supported; it also means that Singapore tertiary institutions have to consider externally defined agendas. A second point: universities may have different missions, and students access university education for different reasons. Many Singaporean students pursue a university education to get themselves prepared for a place in the local/global economy; to lay the foundation for the future; and for some, to pursue learning for learning's sake. These different motivations should clue us into the fact that there may not be a single shared idea or even ideal of the university or what university education is for.

Much as many academics wish to hold on to an ideal, '[t]he university of the future will derive its right to exist primarily from being active *in* the world and by producing knowledge *for* the world' (p. 163). As academics, we have to adjust our role and assume new responsibilities that align better with a changed economy. I am confident that we can do this — academics are the quintessential lifelong learners in our society. In my view, it is more productive to find that delicate balance between making ourselves socially relevant and maintaining our identities as academics. It has been noted that '[s]killed human resources and knowledge resources are two of the most important factors for upgrading national competitive advantage' (Michael Porter, cited in Boulton 2009). The *engaged* university should work with governments and industry to continue to generate knowledge that is socially valued and at the same time '[safeguard] and [protect] innovative and high-stakes research, to avoid the risk of research portfolios becoming too limited as a result of unilateral pressure from societal demand' (p. 180). Again, with reference to Singapore, in the early years of Singapore's history, an important mission of university education was to provide a skilled workforce for nation-building and subsequently for continued national development (see Chan & Chng 2013). In the knowledge economy that characterizes the Singapore economy today, the national impetus to continue to restructure the workforce as it rapidly ages has gained an urgency not seen since those nation-building years. I agree with Van der Zwaan's observation that 'the university may well derive its most important form of legitimacy from its visibility and leadership in society' (p. 182).

In higher education circles, the conversation about research-based education (see Fung 2017) and teaching-led research (Harland 2016), as well as the concept of 'powerful knowledge' (Harland & Wald 2017), may be one way to connect the ivory tower to society. These ideas call for academics to empower all under-graduates to learn by undertaking research so that they cultivate both disciplinary expertise and important life skills. Very often, research is treated as something only senior students can do and is considered beyond the capability of junior undergraduates. But as Harland has shown, re-designing a curriculum that introduces undergraduates to the research process — of formulating questions, developing hypotheses, identifying methods, undertaking data analysis, and responding to critique and feedback — all contribute towards developing critical twenty-first-century skills of critical thinking, evaluation, analysis, and creativity. These skills are exactly the type of competencies that the society needs in confronting an uncertain future. I think as Van der Zwaan does that although 'the university is by no means a sinking ship, … it needs to make a clear about-turn in order to survive' (p. 14), and like all good lifelong learners, academics and academic leaders need to actively participate in its transformation and continued renewal. Change is disorienting, but change can also provide us with the energy to reinvent ourselves. We will need to articulate a broader vision for what we hope to achieve in engaging our society more actively and re-negotiate our roles, for conducting 'business as usual' has its limits and is not responsive to change. For continued relevance and survival, we must deliberate our institutional purpose and role. I hold the view that our institution can function both as ivory tower and as 'national asset'. As intellectual institutions, we are knowledge builders; as social institutions, we shape futures and economies through the education we offer. In their turn, governments and public stakeholders should trust us and honour our integrity as autonomous bodies that are poised between what is needed 'out there' and what we need to do 'from within'. Van der Zwaan wrote: '... the university is actually the most hopeful community that has ever existed, filled with young people who are looking to the future, and clever souls who are opening up new scientific horizons; a community that has shown for the last eight hundred years that it has the resilience to survive' (pp.14-15). We would do well to tap into this 'hopeful community' as we look to the future.

Bibliography

Geoffrey Boulton and Lucas Colin, *What are universities for?* (Brussels: League of European Research Universities, 2008).

Stefan Collini, *What are universities for?* (London: Penguin, 2012)

Daniel S.H. Chan and Huang Hoon Chng ,'Broadening students' experience: A Singapore perspective', in Camille B. Kandiko and Mark Weyers (eds), *The Global Student Experience: An International and Comparative Analysis* (New York: Routledge, 2013), pp. 212-227.

Dilly Fung, *A Connected Curriculum for Higher Education* (London: University College London Press, 2017).

Tony Harland, 'Teaching to enhance research', *Higher Education Research and* Development 35 (3) (2016), pp. 461-472.

Tony Harland and Navé Wald, 'Curriculum, teaching and powerful knowledge', *Higher Education Online*, 3 January 2018, pp. 1-14.

John Newman, *The Idea of a University* (London: Longmans, Green and Co., 1907).

Jaroslav Pelikan, *The Idea of the University – A Reexamination* (New Haven: Yale University Press, 1992).

Hanne Smidt and Andrée Sursock, *Engaging in Lifelong Learning: Shaping Inclusive and Responsive University Strategies* (Brussels: European University Association, 2011).

Harriet Swain, 'What are universities for?', *The Guardian,* 10 October 2011.

Amelia Tang, 'Uni model should develop critical, creative thinking', *The Sunday Times* at A11, 4 February 2018.

Amelia Tang, 'Facing up to challenges in higher education', *The Sunday Times* at A11, 4 February 2018.

Amelia Tang, 'Swopping varsity for "off the beaten track" aspirations', *The Sunday Times* at A11, 4 February 2018.

Bert van der Zwaan, *Higher Education in 2040 — A Global Approach* (Amsterdam: Amsterdam University Press, 2017).

Quality assurance: What it was, is, and should be

Karl Dittrich

Bert van der Zwaan's academic-professional career has developed in parallel with the system of quality assurance in higher education in the Netherlands. From 1986 onwards, Dutch higher education developed a system of evaluation of education and research in response to the government's willingness to grant more autonomy to the higher education sector and to higher education institutions. In this contribution, I will restrict myself to the quality assurance in education.

Originally, the Dutch evaluation system was clearly intended to act as an incentive for the enhancement of quality. However, as soon as the results of the evaluation reports in education became public, the media (especially the newspapers) immediately turned them into rankings. That completely changed the 'innocence' of the evaluation, transforming it into a system of accountability with all consequences.

This emphasis on accountability was reinforced by the introduction in 2002 of a system of programme accreditation, which was the Dutch answer to the requirement of the Bologna process to develop a robust system of internal and external quality assurance in order to build trust between the participatory countries. The Dutch and Flemish governments asked for a system in which an evaluation of the programmes by peers had to be validated by the Dutch-Flemish Accreditation Organisation (NVAO) in order to be funded and to be able to award degrees. One consequence of this change was the introduction of an element of 'fear' in the system, which of course had a huge impact. The higher education institutions calculated their risks and developed internal quality assurance systems that demonstrated that they had done their utmost to be in control of the quality of the programmes. The internal quality systems thus became more focused on procedures and processes than the quality of the content and the outcomes. In addition, staff and students were trained to give the proper answers to questions posed by the evaluation committees.

The robustness of the system took another unlucky turn when incidents came to the fore. A small number of higher education institutions appeared to have problems delivering even the minimal threshold of quality in some programmes. As soon as this was revealed, it led to significant political turmoil and put pressure on the NVAO to become stricter and more rigorous in its quality checks. This has had a devastating effect on the acceptance of the accreditation system by academics. The seeds of mistrust had been planted. Students, politicians, and the media became suspicious and began to question the positive results of the evaluations.

Although the external rules and regulations did not change much, the internal quality assurance systems did. More and more detailed protocols were developed, an increasing amount of data had to be collected, interim evaluations took place, and higher education institutions seemed to be trying to eliminate each and every risk possible. This development is in line with the broader trend we are seeing today towards a risk-free society. In this day and age, mistakes are no longer accepted by politicians or by the general public. More importantly, each mistake is regarded as a failure of the system, irrespective of the sector in which it takes place and of who is responsible. Even when organizations or institutions have been given a large degree of autonomy, faults or mistakes lead to the traditional but unfortunate reflex on the part of the public that such mistakes are 'unacceptable' and that the government must take measures to prevent them from happening again.

Certainly, university administrators have become vulnerable and very much aware of the risk of a loss of prestige and negative publicity. They live in a world of metrics and rankings and are constantly under pressure to ensure that their university does not lose ground. The consequence has been that academic administration has come to resemble a shadow ministry intent on gathering as much data as it can get its hands on. This in turn has led academics to complain about the administration's lack of trust in them and even about encroachments on their 'academic freedom', a holy principle of academia.

Another consequence of administrators' keen interest in 'quality' has been the growth of policy staff involved in quality assurance. In a recently published report of the European Commission on the impact of quality assurance on the quality of teaching and learning, the growth of the number of quality assurance staff was seen as a positive sign of quality improvement. However, one could cast considerable doubt on this conclusion. Quality assurance seems to have become a new 'industry' with its own roles, rules, and culture, which runs the risk of it becoming ever more formalized and all-encompassing.

The administrative burden of quality assurance is currently one of the greatest concerns of academic staff and is seen as one of the main causes of the work overload and stress that many academics (especially the younger ones) experience. Although the need to publish (according to the old axiom 'Publish or perish') and the growing emphasis on global excellence have had negative effects on job satisfaction, academics consider their administrative duties as their number one burden. Universities, governments, quality assurance agencies, politicians, and the media should be much more aware of this situation. Each and every opportunity should be taken to lower the administrative duties of academics, which could also be seen as a necessary step towards restoring trust in the higher education sector. It would also help to direct everyone's attention back to the content of the programmes and away from processes and procedures, which inevitably lead to a box-ticking mentality within all levels of quality assurance.

Is there an alternative to this development I have sketched above? Yes, there is! Instead of focusing on quality assurance, universities could concentrate on developing a quality culture. This idea has recently been getting some attention. While difficult to define and very demanding for universities to cultivate, there are a number of conditions that must be fulfilled before one can speak of a quality culture:

1. Academics must be willing to accept that it is self-evident to watch in the mirror of quality regularly. Science and professions develop continuously, and therefore staff has to be aware that education is dynamic. New insights from research and from the professional world must be incorporated into university programmes in order to ensure that the education they offer remains up to date.

2. Universities must recognize that teaching is one of their key responsibilities. Research is seen as a necessity and still the best way to pursue an academic career, whereas teaching has traditionally been looked upon as a burden. Universities must reaffirm the importance of the quality of teaching and reward it. They should also strive to find a better balance between rewards for research and for teaching.

3. Academics must be self-critical, both on an individual level and as a team. Just as the concept of 'team science' is developing in the field of research, this will lead to changes in the way academics bear their responsibility for education. This self-critical attitude should lead to introspection and to a greater willingness to address each other. It should also encourage universities to invite prestigious peers from other universities to take part in the regular site visits of their programmes.

4. Academics must stay abreast of new pedagogical methods. Learning has changed significantly in recent decades, and so has teaching. Although the teacher-student relationship will remain the main route for acquiring knowledge of a particular discipline, the development of IT, the need to master IT skills for any profession, and the emergence of new gadgets have made education much more a process of developing a professional learning attitude.

5. University managers must show self-confidence when demonstrating how they ensure quality of teaching and learning.

I most certainly am not fond of the concept of earned trust: this concept is based on mistrust, which leads to ever more reports, stringent accountability, and the loss of academic credibility!

There is thus hope for the future, exactly when Bert van der Zwaan is leaving his position as vice-chancellor of Utrecht University. He has been very much aware of the strengths and weaknesses of quality assurance. Without ever denying the need to take a tough stand on the quality of teaching and learning, he has continously sought to look for new ways of convincing the outside world that academia deserves our support and can be trusted. His critical presence in the debate will be missed, but his contributions to discussions about the heart and core of academia will not be forgotten!

Vale rector, vale!

A *Hooge School en Maatschappij* for our time! On the difficult relationship between two types of universities

Leen Dorsman

Universities are extremely self-reflective institutions. At the same time, it is rather rare for a professor or a vice-chancellor to publish extensively on the future of the university itself. Yet Utrecht University has had a tradition of doing exactly that. And recently Bert van der Zwaan has followed the example of his predecessors by publishing his book *Higher Education in 2040 — A Global Approach*. Already in 1831, the professor of history and classical languages Philip Willem van Heusde (1778-1839) wrote his highly successful and influential *Brieven over Hoger Onderwijs* (Letters on Higher Education), which advocated the university as the place where neoclassical *Bildung* should be the core curriculum (no surprise there). Also Gerrit Jan Mulder (1802-1880), one of the founders of modern chemistry in the Netherlands, was active in the debate on general education on the one hand and scientific training on the other. For philosopher and jurist Cornelis Opzoomer (1821-1892) and zoologist Pieter Harting (1812-1885), it was self-evident that they would be involved in discussions on higher education. In the twentieth century, it was the brochure *Hooge School en Maatschappij* (Higher Education and Society) by Hugo Kruyt (1882-1959), a professor of physical chemistry, that resonated for a long time in Dutch academic circles. Bert van der Zwaan is for the time being the last one in this remarkable series.

However interesting it may be to compare Bert van der Zwaan with his nineteenth-century predecessors — who are, as he writes, the pioneers of the research university of today, although some arguments speak against that opinion — a comparison with a twentieth-century colleague, Hugo Kruyt, bears more fruit. The fourth chapter in the book by Van der Zwaan on increasing costs and the possibility (or impossibility) of selection ends with a section entitled 'Why the United States should certainly not be followed'. The reason is that he sees a growing twofold divide in American higher education. On the one hand, there is an increasing gap between the relatively small group of privately financed Ivy League universities and the large group of mass universities dependent on public funding that is barely enough to survive. In the wake of this disastrous (in his eyes) development, he perceives a second, undesired divide: the one between students from lower social strata who have less and less access to higher education and those who have more financial capacities and can afford to study at elite universities. These American trends must indeed not be followed, but in the same paragraph Van der Zwaan asks another important question that perhaps does point us in the direction of American solutions. Considering all the students that enter our universities every year, how many of them are really suited for academic or scientific training? 'At present, many students opt for university than higher vocational education for reasons of status and labour market prospects, rather than because they want a genuinely academic education'. And: 'Why not encourage more students to enter higher vocational education (...)?'

This is not the first time this question has been asked in the context of Utrecht University. For the past twenty years, it has been the subject of many debates. It is a complex question because it is not only about how to 'lead' those students in this direction, it also pertains directly to the relationship between two different types of institutions. It is also a rather controversial question because in Utrecht in particular, the academic university and the universities of applied sciences have for decennia stood with their backs to each other.

This brings me back to Hugo Kruyt and a debate he was involved in in the early 1930s. In 1927, Kruyt visited the United States where he attended conferences and delivered guest lectures at the University of Michigan at Ann Arbor. After returning, he lectured and published articles about his experiences. One lecture he delivered to an Amsterdam-based student society was published in 1931 as a brochure entitled *Hooge School en Maatschappij*. By 'hooge school' he meant university (which is rather confusing nowadays, because we understand 'hogeschool' as university of applied sciences). The structure of the brochure (36 pages only) resembles the structure of Bert van der Zwaan's book. Kruyt also begins his argumentation with a historical analysis of the phenomenon of the university and, like Van der Zwaan, he diagnoses certain problems and shortcomings of his own university and offers some solutions. For Kruyt, the main problem was the inability of the administrators of Dutch universities to understand what the modern university needed. Both Kruyt and Van der Zwaan are conscious of the fact that universities operate in a changing world and therefore must change along with this world or otherwise perish. Both are aware of long-lasting historical developments, but neither idealizes the past. They are both realists.

Yet there is a big difference between *Hooge School en Maatschappij* and *Higher Education in 2040*. This difference has to do mainly with the role of the universities of applied sciences — comparable in many ways to the former polytechnics in the United Kingdom or the *Fachhochschulen* in Germany — or maybe not in their role, but in the position they have in the entirety of higher education. While travelling in the United States, Kruyt keenly observed the way higher education was organized. He noted that the American college system incorporated an endless variation of bachelor programmes 'as a preparation and training for lower intellectual positions'. He called it 'practical diversity'. Students could be trained to be school teachers, hospital nurses, or lab assistants, 'in short: this is training for all positions in society for which a scientific preparation is necessary'. He also speaks of an 'elementary scientific training'. This seemed to him the ideal system: two years of general education, after which followed two years of vocational training. He found out that for

80 per cent of the students, the bachelor's degree meant the end of their stay at the university and that only 20 per cent of them went on to the master's phase. In Kruyt's opinion, this system had three advantages. First, 'the university has and keeps contact with the sparkling life' and was in this way 'a link in the general societal life'. Providing a good education for a broad array of students would benefit the university, because society at large would have a broad appreciation of the university. For Dutch universities in the *interbellum* period, it was precisely this appreciation that was lacking (and the same holds true for the current decade). A second advantage was that it was fairly normal for the bachelor diploma to mean the end of a student's studies. By contrast, in the Netherlands, students with only a 'kandidaats' degree (at that time the equivalent of a bachelor's degree) were seen as university dropouts, while in the United States someone with a bachelor's degree was considered successful. A third attractive element of the American system was the fact that large numbers of students came into contact with scientific ways of thinking and with a general scientific environment.

Seventy years after Kruyt's observations, the Netherlands has a bachelor's and master's system but we have yet to reach the situation in which a substantial part of our students consider the bachelor's degree as the end of studies. The situation Kruyt described was also different from the Dutch system: American students were — and still are — in general younger when they arrive at university. This is why they offer four-year programmes. I am not sure if the American college system is the solution for the problems in our university system, but it is refreshing to read the findings of a colleague who wrote almost a century ago, a colleague who had a sharp eye for the shortcomings of his own university. In his well-balanced book, Bert van der Zwaan touches upon the same set of problems as Hugo Kruyt. I hope that he will continue writing about higher education and one day produce a fine, well-composed brochure on the complex relationship between academic universities and universities of applied sciences: a new *Hooge School en Maatschappij* for our time!

Bibliography

Klaas van Berkel, 'Americanisation of the Dutch university? Chemist H.R. Kruyt about university and society' (in Dutch), *Tijdschrift voor de Geschiedenis der Geneeskunde, Natuurwetenschappen, Wiskunde en Techniek,* 12 (4) (1989), pp. 198-225.

Leen J. Dorsman (ed.), *Appeals to science. Utrecht scholars between university and society, 1850-1940* (in Dutch) (Utrecht: Matrijs, 1999).

Hugo R. Kruyt, *University and Society* (in Dutch) (Amsterdam: Universiteit van Amsterdam, 1931).

Bert Theunissen, *'Utility and again utility' — Conceptions of science of Dutch natural science researchers, 1800-1900* (in Dutch) (Hilversum: Verloren BV, 2000).

Bert van der Zwaan, *Higher Education in 2040 — A Global Approach* (Amsterdam: Amsterdam University Press, 2017).

About the authors

Derrick Anderson is assistant professor at the School of Public Affairs and an advisor to the president of Arizona State University.

Bertil Andersson was provost (2007-2011) and president (2011-2017) of Nanyang Technological University in Singapore and is currently senior advisor at NTU. He is a professor of biochemistry.

Barbara Baarsma is professor of economics at the University of Amsterdam. She is also director of knowledge development at Rabobank.

Alain Beretz is general director for research and innovation at the French ministry for higher education in Paris. He was president of the University of Strasburg from 2008 to 2016. He is a professor of pharmacology.

Huang Hoon Chng is associate provost for undergraduate education at the National University Singapore. Her academic field is English language and literature.

Michael Crow has been president of Arizona State University since 2002 and is professor at the School of Public Affairs at ASU. He has had several senior leadership positions at Columbia University in New York (1992-2002).

Kurt Deketelaere is secretary-general of the League of European Research Universities. He is professor of law at the University of Leuven and also chairman of the Sustainability College in Bruges.

José van Dijck is president of the Royal Netherlands Academy of Arts and Sciences and distinguished university professor at Utrecht University. Her research area is media and culture.

Karl Dittrich is president of the European Quality Assurance Register for Higher Education (EQAR). He is a political scientist and has in the past been president of Maastricht University, of the Accreditation Organisation of the Netherlands and Flanders (NVAO), and of the Association of Dutch Research Universities (VSNU).

Rhea van der Dong is a graduate student in public policy studies at Utrecht University and is president of the Students Council of Dutch Universities (ISO) for the academic year 2017-2018.

Leen Dorsman is distinguished university professor at Utrecht University, with a research focus on the history of universities.

Dilly Fung is director of the Arena Centre for Research-Based Education at University College London. Her research focus is on teaching and learning and the curriculum in higher education.

Armand Heijnen is senior editor in the Corporate Office of Utrecht University and was editor-in-chief of the university's magazine.

James Kennedy is the dean of University College Utrecht, the international liberal arts and sciences college within Utrecht University. He is a professor of modern history.

Jukka Kola has been vice-chancellor of the University of Helsinki since 2013. He is a professor of agricultural policy.

Sari Lindblom is pro-vice-chancellor for teaching and learning at the University of Helsinki and a professor of educational science.

Frank Miedema is the dean of the University Medical Centre of Utrecht. He is a professor of immunology. He is one of the initiators of the 'Science in Transition' initiative.

Anka Mulder is president of Saxion University of Applied Sciences. She is a historian and was also a member of the executive board of Delft University of Technology.

Sijbolt Noorda is president of the Magna Charta Observatory in Bologna. He was president of the University of Amsterdam and of the Association of Dutch Research Universities (VSNU).

Carel Stolker is vice-chancellor of Leiden University. He is a professor of law and also acts as deputy judge.

Joop Schippers is professor of economics at Utrecht University with a focus on labour economics; he is a member of the University Council.

John Sexton served as fifteenth president of New York University, from 2002 to 2015. He is a professor of law and was the dean of NYU's School of Law.

Rob van der Vaart is professor-emeritus in human geography at Utrecht University and was pro-vice-chancellor for education and honours dean at Utrecht University.

Peter Vale is professor of humanities at the University of Johannesburg and director of the Johannesburg Institute for Advanced Study (JIAS).

Kyle Whitman is a PhD student in the School of Public Affairs and a research fellow in the Office of the President at Arizona State University.